THE GREEN-SPACES GUIDE TO LONDON

Published by Verdant Books PO Box 83 NE48 3YY

Printed and bound by Antony Rowe Limited SN14 6LH

British Library cataloguing-in-Publication Data:
A catalogue record for this publication is available from thc British Library

ISBN 0 9535414 1 X

Maps: Redrawn by Verdant Books. Based upon Ordnance Survey mapping.
Acknowledgement: Reproduced by permission of Ordnance Survey on behalf of The Controller of Her Majesty's Stationery Office © Crown Copyright. MC 100033846

Green-Spaces Guide to LONDON

Published by:

VERDANT BOOKS

PO BOX 83, HEXHAM NE48 3YY

WEB: www.green-spaces.co.uk

Tel: 01434 230 489
Fax: 01434 230 725
email: gsguides@green-spaces.co.uk

Acknowledgements
We would like to thank everybody who volunteered information for inclusion in this guide and who supported its creation, without whom it could not have been written.

The site descriptions in the following pages have either come from site visits, or from a description of the garden sent to us from its owner of manager. We are very grateful to all those who want to share their beautiful gardens with fellow enthusiasts.

We know that there are many green spaces in the London area - it has not yet been possible to visit them all. We would love to know about more of them. If you know of any Green Spaces that you think should be - or even should not be - included, please let us know. We will be delighted to post a free copy of the Green-Spaces Guide of your choice to the sender to the first or most interesting letter of any new site

Camley Street Natural Park

ABOUT THIS GUIDE

The guide concentrates in the centre of London, working out towards the M25 and is divided into five mapped areas.

Most of the sites are open regularly (and many are free); **opening times** and specific dates are clearly marked. A few open under the **NGS** (National Gardens Scheme), wherby the admission charge goes to charity. Another anacronym in the text is **SSSI** - Site of Special Scientific Interest, in this instance usually applying to wildlife or wildflower areas.

Acres and Hectares - both may be found, depending on the information we were given. The ratio is
1ha = 2.5 acres (approx.)

The **appendices** at the back of the guide cover some possible areas of interest to the reader - eg sites with historic significance, design, wildlife/wildspace etc.

Please note: opening times refer to the green-space only - **not** to an accompanying building.
Wheelchair access - assume that wheelchair access is adequate, unless it is otherwise stated.
In all cases - if in doubt - 'phone!

INTRODUCTION

What do you want from the green spaces around you? A gentle stroll in a park, a quiet corner to relax on a sunny day? To further your horticultural knowledge?

The aim of this guide is to give you this spectrum of opportunities to enjoy the green spaces in London - there are more of them here than almost any other city in Europe. Parks, gardens and garden squares, heathland, arboreta, nurseries and garden centres.

Sites in this guide can range from the expected to the obscure - Hyde Park, Hampstead Heath, Regent's Park, Kew, all to be expected; but what about the Victorian 'Jurassic Park' at Crystal Palace, the modernist design for the Thames Barrier Park, and a 1½ acre roof garden, high above Kensington High Street?

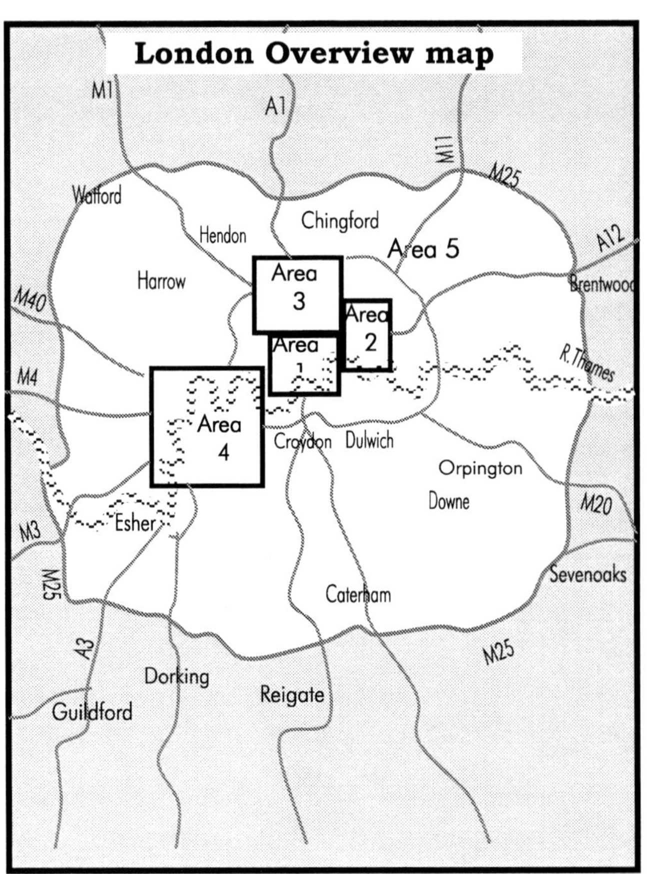
London Overview map
M1
A1
M11
M25
Watford
Hendon
Chingford
Area 5
A12
Harrow
Area 3
Brentwood
M40
Area 2
Area 1
R.Thames
M4
Area 4
Croydon
Dulwich
Orpington
Downe
M20
Esher
M3
M25
Sevenoaks
Caterham
M25
A3
Dorking
Reigate
Guildford

CONTENTS

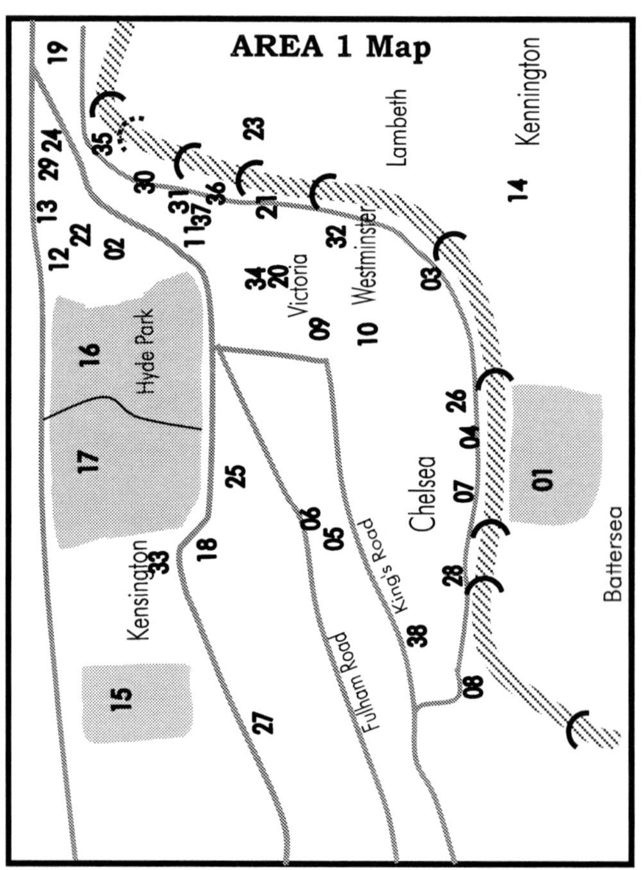
AREA 1 Map
Kennington
Lambeth
Westminster
Victoria
Hyde Park
Chelsea
Kensington
King's Road
Fulham Road
Battersea
19
35
23
24
29
30
31
36
37
11
21
13
22
02
12
32
14
03
34
20
09
10
16
26
04
17
25
07
01
06
05
18
33
28
38
08
15
27

AREA 1 - Hyde Park, Westminster, Lambeth, Battersea, Chelsea, Kensington

01. BATTERSEA PARK

(Wandsworth Borough Council)

8am - dusk

Prince of Wales Drive, Battersea SW11 Tel: 0208 871 7572

A 200 acre Victorian park, opened in 1858. Many features, including two lakes, one natural in style with a rocky cascade and informal planting, the other formal, with fountains, part of 'The Grand Vista'. There is an 'Old English Garden', a herb garden, and many statues and sculptures, from Victorian to Modern. The Horticultural Therapy Garden holds daily demonstrations, and is laid out to show how to make gardening easier for disabled people. Please note that the Park is currently undergoing a major regeneration, with new and restoration projects in progress.

WC. Café. Children's play areas & adventure playground. Train: Battersea Park

02. BERKELEY SQUARE GARDENS

(City of Westminster)

daily

W1

Berkeley Square is famed for two reasons. The first, the nightingale which sang there, according to the song lyrics and the second, the plane trees, some of which are amongst the oldest in central London. There is a nymph statue (originally a drinking fountain!) at the south end, and a 'covered shelter' in the centre of the garden. There are some handsome tubs containing cones of box and seasonal bedding

03. BESSBOROUGH GARDENS

(City of Westminster)
8am - dusk
Vauxhall Bridge Road SW1
A one acre site just off the busy Vauxhall Bridge Road. Soil mounding and shrub planting combined with the gentle sound from the large fountain at one end distract from the hubub outside. Varied planting and different types of paving contribute to give the site individuality. Pity about the skyscraper emerging opposite.
Tube: Pimlico

04. CHELSEA EMBANKMENT GARDENS

(The Royal Borough of Kensington and Chelsea)
daily
Chelsea Embankment SW3
A serpentine path wends through pleasant gardens alongside the busy Chelsea Embankment. Spring and summer bedding, trees and broad grass areas. A shrub bed banks up one side, and memorials punctuate its length. There are views over the Thames and pretty Albert Bridge.

05. CHELSEA GARDENER, THE

10am - 6pm mon - sat; 12 - 6pm suns.

Chelsea Farmers Market, 125 Sydney Street SW3 Tel: 0207 352 5656

Plush and expensive garden centre. A choice range of plants from trees to seasonal bedding (all in the best possible taste, of course), lovely pots, garden furniture and sundries. Much of the centre is under a canopy cover. The right place to plant up the window box of your Georgian town house.

Tube: Sloane Square + 12 mins walk

06. CHELSEA GREEN (CHELSEA COMMON)

(The Royal Borough of Kensington and Chelsea)

daily

Cale Street SW3

A small triangular site, mainly in because of its historical interest; it is the remnant of what was Chelsea Common. Two cherry trees, the older one of which stands over benches and borders of seasonal bedding.

07. CHELSEA PHYSIC GARDEN

(Trustees of Chelsea Physic Garden)

April - October, Wednesdays 12 - 5pm & Sundays 2 - 6pm ONLY. Also open every day during Chelsea Flower Show Week in May 12 - 5pm & Chelsea Festival Week in June 12 - 5pm.

66 Royal Hospital Road SW3 4HS Tel: 0207 352 5646

London's 'Secret Garden'. A real feast for the plantsperson, with a history going back to 1673, when it was founded by the Society of Apothecaries. Many rare, tender and unusual plants grow in its four acres, both outside in borders and order beds, and inside in its variety of glasshouses. Most of these are wood-framed and have a variety of climates, from steamy tropical to temperate. There is also a cool fern house in another area of the garden, which houses many ferns and has a small moisture-laden case for filmy ferns at one end. The garden holds the National Collection of cistus, and also has a very old Olive tree (Olea europea) which at 30 feet is the largest growing outside in the UK. The garden continues to maintain its research associations.

Entrance via Swan Walk. Admission: Adults: £4; Children (5-15yrs), Students & unemployed (with ID): £2; Toilets/and for disabled; Tea room; Tube: Sloane Square + 15 mins walk

08. CREMORNE GARDENS

(The Royal Borough of Kensington and Chelsea)

7.30am - dusk

Lots Road SW10

This site was part of a larger area of garden, now built upon, and has managed to retain no sense of history apart from the huge, beautifully made and restored cast iron gates which stand alone in the middle of the gardens. The gates divide an informal grass area from the raised beds and cobble paths which lead to a riverside walkway and short pier.

09. EBURY SQUARE GARDEN

(City of Westminster)

8am until variable evening closing.

Buckingham Palace Road SW1

Tranquil small square laid out in the usual way, but with more interesting planting and 'extra' features, such as the working fountain in the centre surrounded by standard eleagnus and a soothing colour scheme of white, yellow and blue.

Tube: Sloane Square

10. ECCLESTON SQUARE

(The Residents of Eccleston Square. Garden Manager: Roger Phillips)

ONLY open 1 day per year (for NGS)

Belgrave Road, Pimlico SW1 Tel:0207 834 7354

Wonderful 2.9 acre garden near the centre of London, full of rare and interesting plants. This includes an NCCPG collection of Ceanothus (56 different varieties), 110 camellias, more than 400 different roses, including some wild Chinese species, a Handkerchief or Ghost Tree (Davidia involucrata) and many other unusual trees and shrubs.

Admission: Adults £2; Children & OAP's £1. Plants for sale. Teas. Train/ Tube: Victoria.

11. GREEN PARK

(Royal Parks Agency)

daily

Piccadilly

An unpretentious name for what is, literally, 53 acres of green park. The greens of the grass and canopy of trees (of which there are many) is broken by seasonal changes, drifts of bulbs in the spring and the yellows and reds of autumn.

12. GROSVENOR SQUARE

(Royal Parks Agency)
daily 7.30am - dusk
W1
The design and layout of this London Square results in a sophisticated park area, which has had strong links with the US since the 1930's - indeed the US Embassy stands along one length of the Square. A wide path creates a strong central axis, linking the British memorial to President Roosevelt to that of the Eagle Squadron, both dignified and sensitive works of art. Beautiful stonework on low walls and paving, crisp delineating hedges, unfussy, attractive planting and tidy lawns, set the tone for this elegant London Square.

13. HANOVER SQUARE

(City of Westminster)
daily
W1
Pretty, small London square with paths radiating out from the centre. Clipped evergreens around the outside, nicely planted tubs and borders within.

14. HARLEYFORD ROAD COMMUNITY GARDEN

daily 9am - dusk

Harleyford Road, Vauxhall SW8 Tel: 0207 735 0479

¾ ha community garden with an eclectic mix of planting types. Wildlife is encouraged with a pond, nature trail and walkways.

Childrens play area. Tube: Vauxhall or Oval.

15. HOLLAND PARK

(The Royal Borough of Kensington and Chelsea)

7.30am - dusk

Ilchester Place W8 Tel: 0207 471 9813

50 acre gardens with a 400 year old history around Holland House. From the car park you first reach the formal Dutch Garden, originally laid out in 1812. It is a large parterre with box hedging and seasonal bedding. Shrub borders around the edge contain a fine selection of unusual plants. The Azalea Walk is stunning in May, and takes you past the Arboretum. This contains mature and specimen trees, many planted 100-200 years ago. There are said to be approximately 3000 different species of plants in the Park. Near the Orangery is the Dahlia garden, and also a Camellia border: in fact, there are many areas of interest throughout the year.

Some labelling. Toilets/and for disabled. Restaurant & Café. Children's adventure playground. Tube: Holland Park + 10 mins walk

Holland Park- KYOTO GARDEN

A one acre Japanese garden within Holland Park, donated by the Chamber of Commerce of Kyoto in 1991. A waterfall cascades through rock into a pool which in turn tumbles into the small lake which meanders through the site. Although bright in spring with azaleas and pieris, it is, as a Japanese garden should be, carefully proportioned and tranquil.

16. HYDE PARK

(Royal Parks Agency)

dawn - dusk

Hyde Park Corner SW1 Tel: 0207 298 2000

Huge green space, right in the heart of London; 350 acres of grass, lake, woodland and meadow. It is a reflection of British cultural identity, that such a large piece of open land has been kept so close to the centre of the capital city; that it is such an uninteresting open space is disappointing. The 'Rose Garden', 'Dell' and Serpentine are features, and the area around the Hudson Memorial is quiet and contemplative. Don't bother looking for the 'Reformers Tree', the place where the first public meetings were allowed - there is no tree, just a commemorative plaque set into the tarmac. Maybe they couldn't decide on which tree specie to plant. However, the park makes an excellent outdoor recreation area, and is much used for walking, cycling, roller-blading and horse-riding.

Toilets/and for disabled. Tea rooms. Cycling. Horse riding. Map available from Hyde Park Corner info. Centre. Tube: Hyde Park Corner.

Hyde Park - THE DELL
As its name implies, it is a steeply sloping wooded site, of about an acre, which acts as a dam for one end of the Serpentine. It is wooded with acers, rhododendrons and azaleas amongst others, and gives the impression of a Japanese or Scottish west coast garden. A stream gushes down the 'hillside', with marginal planting along the edges.

Hyde Park - THE ROSE GARDEN
Recently established rose garden. From the east end, you are led from an intimate circular rose garden with a fountain in the centre and herbaceous plants mixed with roses in the surrounding borders, where pillars joined by rope swags stand above; down a path of more mixed rose and herbaceous borders protected on one side by young espaliered limes. At the far end there is a rose pergola. Labelling is quite good.

17. KENSINGTON GARDENS
(Royal Parks Agency)
dawn - dusk
Kensington Gore
Originally part of Hyde Park, Kensington Gardens are nearly 300 acres of Park and Garden. It has been developed during the past 300 years by and for various members of the Royal Family. The Diana Memorial Children's playground is at the Bayswater end of the

gardens, and is all the playground that children and parents could wish for.
Tube: High Street Kensington

Kensington Gardens - THE LOGGIA & ITALIAN GARDEN
Victorian Italianate loggia (disguising the pumphouse) stands above the formal water gardens of five pools and fountains, which cascade down into the 'Long Water' at the far end. A pity that this 'garden' is not more enclosed, as the surrounding parkland distracts the eye.

Kensington Gardens - The Sunken Garden

Kensington Gardens - THE SOUTH FLOWER WALK

The South Flower Walk is a pretty tarmac walk with mixed flowering shrubs and seasonal bedding on either side.

Kensington Gardens - THE SUNKEN GARDEN & ORANGERY

Formal sunken garden surrounded by a lime allée which has 'windows' cut into it at regular intervals so that you can see down into the garden. Terraces of herbaceous plants and colourful bedding drop down to a rectangular pool, in which three fountains play. From the far end of the 'Sunken Garden' a vista leads up to the Queen Anne Orangery, accentuated by 16 magnificent columns of bay and holly.

Guide dogs only. Tea room/restaurant in Orangery

18. KENSINGTON ROOF GARDEN

(The Virgin Group)

10am - 5pm if not in use - 'phone to check

99 High Street, Kensington W8 Tel: 0207 937 7994

At 1½ acres, this is the largest roof garden in Europe, designed in the 1930's by Ralph Hancock above what was Derry & Toms department store. To find a garden as interesting as this in the centre of London would be nice, but to find it 100 feet up on the roof of what was a department store is incredible! Native and exotic plants grow here in the three different areas of garden - the shady woodland garden, walled Tudor garden and formal Spanish garden. Pools and cascades, and a

variety of trees and shrubs are to be found here - and don't miss the flamingos!
No Picnics. Tube: High Street Kensington

19. LINCOLN'S INN FIELDS

(London Borough of Camden)
daily 7.30am - dusk
High Holborn WC2 Tel: 0207 974 1693
The largest of London's square's, Lincoln's Inn Fields has been a public open space for at least 800 years. Currently, it is a large open space, with unusual trees and shrubs as well as some splendid specimens of London Plane tree. A bandstand in the centre is surrounded by a large hard standing area, useful for seating whilst the band concerts are on in the summer. There is a small subtropical garden on one side of the park, where a selection of frost tender plants are growing outside - Agave, tree ferns, Echium, Dizygothica and more.
Toilets. Café. Tube: Holborn

20. LOWER GROSVENOR GARDEN

(City of Westminster)
10am until variable late afternoon closing.
SW1
A small site that just takes you away from the hustle of Victoria Station and its environs. Plane trees shelter many benches allowing the visitor to rest and enjoy the seasonal bedding inside a formal design of lavender hedging punctuated by topiary box and yew cones. A

pair of small pebble-encrusted buildings, 'shell-houses', mark either end of one of the paths across it.

21. MILLBANK GARDEN

(City of Westminster)

daily

John Islip Street SW1

Pretty, sunken rectangular gardens of ½ acre, in a quiet residential area. Colourful shrubs and good seasonal bedding.

22. MOUNT STREET GARDEN

(City of Westminster)

8am - dusk; 9am suns & b'hols.

Mayfair W1

This is not a large park, but there are an awful lot of benches within it - I counted 87 - there may be more. Despite the seating for about 300 people, the gardens are quiet and peaceful, and the benches are rather more a vector for self expression as almost every one of them has a dedication, generally to the peace and beauty of the gardens. This neighbourhood, near Grosvenor Square and the US Embassy is well populated with Americans, and judging from the majority of the benches, they love these gardens. These sheltered and enclosed gardens have mature plane trees, a small grove of Dawn Redwoods, (Metasequoia) and a wonderful Acacia tree, a tower of yellow flowers in the spring, and borders well planted with a variety of shrubs, herbaceous and annual plants.

23. MUSEUM OF GARDEN HISTORY

(The Tradescant Trust)

Open from February - December, daily 10.30am - 5pm

St. Mary-at-Lambeth, By Lambeth Palace, Lambeth Palace Road SE1 7LB Tel: 0207 401 8865

A well kept enclosed garden created from the churchyard behind the church of St Mary-at-Lambeth, now this unique Museum. Plants that would be found growing in the UK in the C17th surround the knot garden, which was designed by Lady Salisbury of Hatfield House. An 8' spiral of golden holly punctuates the centre. There are other topiary features in the garden. The Tradescants were prolific plant collectors, father and son, both of whom are buried in the churchyard in a fine tomb, next to that of Admiral Bligh of the Bounty.

Café. Gift Shop. Train/ Tube: Waterloo + 507 bus.

24. PHOENIX COMMUNITY GARDEN

daily 7.30am - dusk

21 Stacey Street WC2H 8DG Tel: 0207 379 3187

This garden of ½ acre provides a haven for wildlife, the local community and passers by, giving them a slice of the countryside in the heart of the city. There is a woodland area, pergola and the back of the garden is currently being redesigned. Various types of planting survive the poor, dry soil to provide interest for its wide spectrum of users, including an Umbrella Fern, a direct descendent of the one brought back from the

South Pacific by Charles Darwin. Local outside events are held here too.
No dogs. Children's play area. Tube: Tottenham Court Road; Leicester Square.

25. PIRELLI GARDEN

(Victoria & Albert Museum)
daily except 24-25 Dec
Cromwell Road SW7
It is nice on a hot day to rest your eyes and legs in this simple plaza within the V&A. Shallow steps radiate out from the fountain and basin opposite the garden doors, and cypress trees give some shade. An Italian-style garden, reflecting both thc architecture and the main sponsor of the garden.
Garden is accessed through museum - £5 admission. WC. Tube: South Kensington

26. RANELAGH GARDENS

(Royal Hospital, Chelsea)
10-12 & 2-4pm mon - sat; 2 - 4 suns. Closed Christmas and New Year and also for 6 weeks May - June due to Chelsea Flower Show, which spreads into it from Royal Hospital South Grounds.
Chelsea Bridge Road Tel: 0207 730 0161
This undulating rectangular site to the west of busy Chelsea Bridge Road was formerly the Pleasure Grounds of Ranelagh. Wide paths wend through a variety of mature trees and shrubs. Near the garden entrance is a summerhouse designed by Sir John Soane.

Entrance through Royal Hospital Main Gates. Tube: Sloane Square + 7 mins walk

27. RASSELL'S NURSERY

9am - 5.30pm mon - sat; 11am - 5.30pm sundays.
The Lodge Nursery, 78-80 Earls Court Road W8 6EQ Tel: 0207 937 0481

A west end nursery started in the 1890's, which continues to develop its interest in plants rather than horticultural sundries. Specialities include herbaceous plants, roses and indoor plants, especially orchids. There is also a broad range of general shrubs and trees, cut flowers, christmas trees, and imported handmade terracotta pots from Tuscany.
Tube: Earls Court

28. ROPERS GARDENS

(The Royal Borough of Kensington and Chelsea)
7.30am - dusk
Cheyne Walk SW3

A clean-cut garden designed on two levels. Simple planting, chosen for its foliage and form on the walls and in the borders.
The garden is just to the east of Battersea Bridge on the north side.

29. SOHO SQUARE

(City of Westminster)
daily
W1

Pretty, informal London square of just over one acre. Quaint mock-Tudor shelter. Mixture of mature trees, some well planted tubs and good seasonal bedding.

30. ST JAMES' SQUARE

(St. James' Square Trust)

mon - fri 8am - 4.30pm. Closed Weekends

SW1

The earliest London square, started in 1665. Medium sized area, laid out in fairly standard London Square design, but with a different impression, brought about by its private ownership. The large statue in the centre is semi-hidden by a double ring of mixed shrub and herbaceous beds, phormiums and fatsias, roses and cistus, and seating is tucked away off the paths. This type of planting is echoed in the border inside the perimeter fence. A classical-style pavillion stands at one end.

Tube: Piccadilly Circus

31. ST JAMES'S PARK

(Royal Parks Agency)

Dawn - dusk

The Mall SW1A

Famous park facing Buckingham Palace. Due to its proximity to the Houses of Parliament it is one of the few places where politcians and pelicans intermingle. The site is linear, with the longest length running along The Mall. The Park is natural in style, with lawns broken by clumps of trees, winding paths, flower beds,

and the five acre lake which sweeps through the middle. It is immaculately kept. The Geranium bed, for instance is deadheaded daily, and dead plants are removed in the early hours of the morning. There are many exotic and ornamental birds living here, the most decorative being the aforementioned pelicans. The park is much used in the summer by office workers and tourists alike.
Children's playground. Café. Toilets

32. ST JOHN'S GARDENS

(City of Westminster)
8am - dusk
Horseferry Road SW1
Original 1880's layout sheltered by the overhead branches of plane trees. A hornbeam hedge defines a circular pool and fountain in the centre, from which york stone paths radiate out like the points of a compass. Each grass area in between the paths contains a bed of seasonal plants and there are shrubberies and new plantings around the edges of the garden. The staff room is disguised as a classiacal gazebo. The site has recently had a major refurbishment with new lighting, railings and gates.
Tube: Pimlico

33. ST MARY ABBOTS & ALEC CLIFTON TAYLOR MEMORIAL GARDENS

(The Royal Borough of Kensington and Chelsea)
7.30am - dusk
Kensington Church Street W8

Secluded behind the church of St Mary Abbots and bustling Kensington High Street, this is an 'L'-shaped site with roses and seasonal bedding. One bar of the 'L' has a brick-and-timber pergola covered with clematis and roses.
Tube: High Street Kensington

34. UPPER GROSVENOR GARDEN
daily 10 am until variable late afternoon closing
SW1
Recently revamped small garden, the mirror site to 'Lower Grosvenor Garden'. The refurbishment includes a wonderful new statue, new planting and railings.

35. VICTORIA EMBANKMENT GARDENS
(City of Westminster)
7.30am - dusk
Villiers Street WC2
A charming set of gardens immaculately maintaining their Victorian civic gardening roots.
Train: Charing Cross. Tube: Embankment

Victoria Embankment Gardens - MAIN GARDENS
Villiers St. WC2
A long and irregular shaped site, which, if you enter from the west gate, funnels down from a wide formal area with topiary (including a flower basket as a centre piece), and good seasonal bedding, to a path that winds through shrub filled borders interspersed with a variety of artefacts donated by and/or in memory of

'worthies', including one statue of Robbie Burns, and another of Arthur Sullivan.
Tea room

Victoria Embankment Gardens - THE WHITEHALL GARDENS
Horseguards Avenue SW1

Gravel paths allow you to perambulate around this long rectangular site, dominated at the east end by two magnificent Catalpa's (Indian Bean Tree). Three large statues of different 'worthies' punctuate the length, with beds of good seasonal bedding. Mature shrub and tree borders enclose the site.

The Whitehall Gardens

36. VICTORIA TOWER GARDENS SOUTH

(City of Westminster)
daily
Millbank SW1
Plain gardens beside the Houses of Westminster, a useful place for sightseers to rest tired feet. Pleasant views across the Thames, and some good statuary.

37. WESTMINSTER ABBEY

(Dean and Chapter of Westminster)
Tues, Weds & Thurs ONLY, 10am - 6pm (4pm closing on Weds & from Oct - March)
Westminster Abbey SW1 Tel: 0207 222 5152

Westminster Abbey - LITTLE CLOISTER GARDEN

A light garden to be looked at from the darkness of the surrounding cloister. Tranquil and traditional, with a simple colour scheme of green and white, and a fountain in the centre.

Westminster Abbey - THE COLLEGE GARDEN

In the refined periphery of Westminster Abbey is one of the oldest gardens in the U.K. In cultivation since the 11th Century, it is now a large grass area, parkland-like with a few mature plane trees. Around the edges are a selection of planting types. On one side of the entrance to the garden from the cloister, is a recently planted selection of botanically interesting plants; on the other side, a formal garden of topiary and gravel. The herb garden links the site to its past, where

medicinal plants would have been grown for use in the infirmary. At the south end the planting is more woodland-style, surrounding a seating area. Behind this is the beautiful statue of 'The Crucifiction' by Enzo Plazotta.
20p donation welcomed.

38. WORLD'S END NURSERIES

9am - 6pm mon - sat; 10am - 5pm Sunday
441-457 Kings Road SW10 Tel: 0207 351 3343
A one acre garden centre site on King's Road selling a wide range of plants and associated products, including Italian terracotta pots.

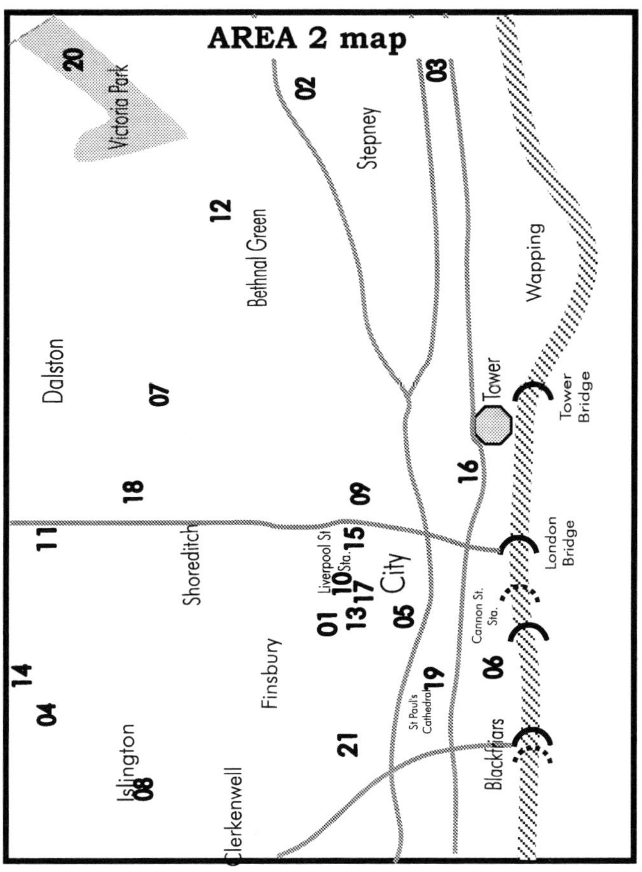
AREA 2 map
Victoria Park
20
02
03
Stepney
12
Bethnal Green
Dalston
07
Wapping
Tower
Tower Bridge
18
09
16
11
Shoreditch
Liverpool St Sta.
10
15
City
17
13
01
05
London Bridge
Cannon St. Sta.
06
19
St Paul's Cathedral
14
04
Finsbury
21
Islington
08
Blackfriars
Clerkenwell

AREA 2 - Bethnal Green, The City, Islington

01. BARBICAN CENTRE

(Corporation of London)
daily
Silk Street EC2

A large complex of offices and flats around the main arts centre. It was all built to one plan, so the site has a unified interpretation. 20km of well-tended window boxes soften the architecture, as do the various gardens around it. The Highwalk is the system of wide paths or walkways, so called because they are above street level. Beware - the Barbican is like a maze, and the direction boards are worth looking out for.
Tube: Barbican

Barbican Centre - CONSERVATORY

Open week-ends & bank hols, but phone to check, as it is sometimes closed for maintenance. Large windows for viewing from the Highwalk at other times.

Huge conservatory on different levels, containing many frost tender plants, from palms to cacti. The height of the conservatory allows plants to become their full height, hence ordinary Ficus benjamina becomes a tree, as does Ficus bengalensis and the pair of dove-grey Cupressus cashmiriana, that greet you as you enter. Bougainvillea and the Swiss Cheese plant, Monstera deliciosa are rampant,Tillandsia drapes from trees, and Billbergia spill out from baskets. The Tropics in the centre of London!

Barbican Centre - BARBER SURGEONS HALL
Wood Street EC2
Small herb garden on the west side of the Barber Surgeons Hall. There is also a small parterrre on the south side of the building, which, when viewed for this book, was planted up with pink daisies, and gave the impression of a persian carpet cut into the lawn.

Barbican Centre - BEECH GARDENS
above Beech Street
Part of the Highwalk. Paviors sweep up to form raiscd beds with shrubs and ground cover, bulbs and seasonal bedding.

Barbican Centre - ST ALPHAGE GARDENS
Fore Street E1
Split level site. Top garden level has a section of London Wall, built by the Romans in 200AD. A large magnolia dominates this area, and stands above a wooden staircase, descending to the lower garden. Here, terraces of shrubs and seasonal bedding drop down from Fore Street above.

Barbican Centre - ST ALPHAGE HIGHWALK GARDENS
London Wall EC2

A small roof garden, part of the Highwalk system. Raised beds and trellis are planted up with an emphasis on form and texture.

Barbican Centre - ST GILES' CHURCH

London Wall

This charming church fronts onto the remarkable lake system which runs through the Barbican. This water feature, canal-like, with weirs, is a stunning piece of architecture and civil engineering.

02. BEAUMONT SQUARE GARDENS

(London Borough of Tower Hamlets)

8am - dusk

Stepney E1

A pretty, quiet London square just off the busy Mile End Road, overlooked by mixed housing. An axial design, with a 10' standard magnolia in the centre. Paths leading to this are lined with seasonal bedding, but more informal planting towards the edges of the garden divides it up into quiet seating areas.

Children's play area. Tube: Stepney Green

03. CABLE STREET COMMUNITY GARDENS

Hardinge St/ Cable Street E1 Tel: 0207 480 5456

Community Garden established in the 1970's. Local residents are key-holders to more than 50 plots, which reflect the wide diversity of age, backgrounds and nationalities. Fruit, flowers, vegetables, wildflowers and hedgerows are all grown according to the tastes of the different plot holders - but organic gardening

principles are used throughout the site. A herb garden is being developed at the front. The project has been so successful, a 'seedling' garden has ben set up at Glamis Road Community Gardens.
Tube: Shadwell.

04. CANONBURY SQUARE

(London Borough of Islington)
daily 8am - dusk
N1
Neat and charming small London Square in a formal style. Low raised beds with colourful bedding are interspersed with the evergreen palm 'Cordyline'. A few evergreen and deciduous trees soften the boundary fence.

05. CHURCHYARD OF ST JOHN ZACHARY

(Worshipful Company of Goldsmiths)
daily
Gresham St EC2
Split level garden. Top level is like a tiny woodland, where bark paths twist around a central plane tree. This overlooks a formal sunken garden, whose walls are covered in climbers, surrounding a square of grass and fountain.

06. CLEARY GARDENS

(Corporation of London)
daily
Queen Victoria Street EC4

Interesting garden in the shadow of St Paul's Cathedral. A long brick and timber loggia runs parallel to busy Queen Victoria Street and the garden slopes away from this. The site is divided into different levels and areas mainly through the use of steps and climber-covered wooden pergolas. Shrubs and herbaceous plants edge the paths.

07. COLUMBIA ROAD FLOWER MARKET

Sundays 8am-2pm

Columbia Road, near Bethnal Green E2

If you like things 'plant', get up early on a Sunday morning and go to this wonderful and fun market. Every type of plant can be found; lots of houseplants, cacti, bulbs, perennials, cut flowers and florists materials. Other garden related stalls and shops are gathering around the market, selling pots and arty garden items.

Tube: Shoreditch

08. CULPEPPER COMMUNITY GARDEN

10am - 5pm

1 Cloudesley Road, Islington N1 0EJ Tel: 0207 833 3951

Much is fitted into this award-winning ¾ acre site. 2 ponds, a pergola and communal flower beds unite the garden, which has 46 plots used by individuals, families, schools and other local organisations. Organic principles are used throughout the site.

Plants for sale. No dogs allowed. Tube: Angel

09. CUTLER STREET GARDENS

daily 8am - 8pm

Cutler Street E1 Tel: 0207 626 8373

Designed by Russell Page, these series of interlinked courtyard gardens surround Cutler Gardens offices. These are towering buildings of polished pink granite. This material is brought down to earth, literally, as pink portugese granite setts sweep through and unify the site. Water features in most of the courtyards in imaginative forms of fountain, pool and cascade. The planting, is carefully thought out, as only such an elegant and restrained result can be.

Train/ Tube: Liverpool Street

10. FINSBURY CIRCUS

(Corporation of London)

1 May - 30 Sept. 8am - dusk. Oct - April weekdays only.

EC2

The largest public open space in the City, which may be a result of being London's first public park, opened in 1606. As well as being home to the City of London Bowling Club, there are also shrub borders, seasonal bedding, many fine old Plane trees and unique to the City, a Pagoda Tree (Sophora japonica) at the corner of the Bowling Green.

11. GEFFRYE MUSEUM HERB GARDEN

(Trustees of the Geffrye Museum)

Tues - Sat 10am - 5pm, Sunday, Bank hol. Mons 2 -

5pm. Closed mondays (except bank hols), Good Friday, 24 - 26 Dec & 1st Jan
Kingsland Road E2 5EA Tel: 0207 739 9893
50' x 50' square, it contains over 170 herbs in beds intersected by geometric paths in the style of monastic gardens, with a well-head at the centre. The herbs are planted by use, including cosmetic, medicinal and household herbs. This Award winning garden is brought to life through drama, music, workshops and seminars. There are also the 'Period Garden Rooms', a major feature which links the domestic theme of interiors within the Museum, with the exterior garden space outside. Hence there are examples of a late C16th knot garden; Elizabethan herbal garden; an ornamental Georgian garden of the mid C18th; a Regency 'Rosarie' and flower garden; Victorian garden and Edwardian Arts & Crafts influence garden. All the gardens reflect examples of town gardens which may have been found at that time.
WC in museum. Tube: Old Street.

12. MUSEUM GARDENS
(London Borough of Tower Hamlets)
daily dawn - dusk
Cambridge Heath Road E2
Pretty medium sized park, next to the Museum of Childhood in Bethnal Green. Lots of well kept grass, evergreen and deciduous trees including some nice specimen conifers, shrubberies and seasonal bedding.
Tube: Bethnal Green

13. MUSEUM OF LONDON

Easter - October Mon - Sat 10am - 5.50 pm, Sunday 12pm - 5.50pm

London Wall EC2Y 5HN Tel: 0207 600 3699

Designed courtyard garden chronologically displaying plant introductions to London from Medieval times to the present day.

Admission: Adults £4; Concessions £2; Family Ticket £9.50. Charge includes entry to museum, permanent galleries and temporary exhibitions. Tube: St Paul's; Barbican.

14. NEW RIVER WALK

(London Borough of Islington)

weekdays 8am dusk (9am sats; 10am suns)

Canonbury Rd N1

New River Walk

This is not actually a river, but rather a slim, man-made aqueduct, built between 1609-1613 to bring fresh drinking water from Hertfordshire to London. It was a great engineering feat of its time, keeping almost to the same level for most of its 38 mile route. The prettiest stretch from Canonbury Road to Islington was restored from 1996-98 and is the result of hard work from both the local residents and the Council. You can now walk alongside the canal on gravel paths which wend their way through a well landscaped narrow park. The planting and layout of the area is such that it is lovely at any time of the year.
o dogs. Tube: Canonbury

15. ST BOTOLPH WITHOUT BISHOPSGSATE

(Corporation of London)
daily
Bishopsgate EC2
A sheltered garden just south of Liverpool Street Station. Use is made of its microclimate to grow some slightly tender plants well, Convolvulus cneorum, bay and abutilon, for example. Facing onto the garden, the Church Hall has two charming Coate Stone figurines.

16. ST DUNSTAN IN THE EAST

(Corporation of London)
daily
St. Dunstan's Hill EC3
Beautifully romantic in the sense of human endeavours being so frail. One of Wren's finest

churches was bombed out in WW2. It is now a secret green space, where walls are covered in vines and creepers, rampant in clematis and appropriately, passion flower (so named because parts of the flower were thought to have biblical symbolism to do with the crucifixion). Borders run around the edges and up to the walls, and contain a variety of interesting plants including azara, acacia and hydrangea.

17. ST MARY ALDERMANBURY

(Corporation of London)

daily

Love Lane EC2

This ruined Wren church is marked out with low walls of clipped box, yew and shrub borders. A Magnolia grandiflora towers above the Victorian style knot garden, which is filled with seasonal bedding and a 20'+ Swamp Cypress (Taxodium ditichum) stands to one side. A tall yew hedge encloses a small secret garden, where a bust of William Shakespeare is protected by camellia's, ruscus, rubus and mahonia.

18. ST MARY'S GARDEN

Mon - Fri 10am - 4pm & occasional Saturday's

Pearson St., Hackney E2 Tel: 0207 739 2965

One acre Horticultural Therapy garden run by 'Thrive' for disabled people and those with additional needs. Herbs, fruit, veg. and sensory planting.

Plants for sale. Toilets/ and for disabled. Tube: Old Street.

19. ST PAUL'S CATHEDRAL GARDEN

daily
EC4
Any garden that sits below stupendous St Paul's Cathedral is going to diminshed. However there is a pretty rose garden on the south side with roses in beds and also climbing over the railings. A large Fremontodendron benefits from being against a south-facing wall. There are other gardens around the Cathedral, lawns with trees and shrubs on the North, and shrub borders abutting the rose garden.

20. VICTORIA PARK

(London Borough of Tower Hamlets)
daily dawn - dusk
Grove Road, South Hackney
Large (218 acres) Metropolitan Park divided in two by Grove Road. Shrub and herbaceous borders on the west side sweep down to the lake, from which emerges a water spout. A bandstand is on the east.
Children's play areas. Toilets & for disabled. Café by lake.
Train: Cambridge Heath

21. WEST SMITHFIELD

(Corporation of London)
daily
EC1
A circular garden at the end of a radial axis from The Old Bailey and Smithfield Market. A statue in the centre is surrounded by urns, trees and shrubs.

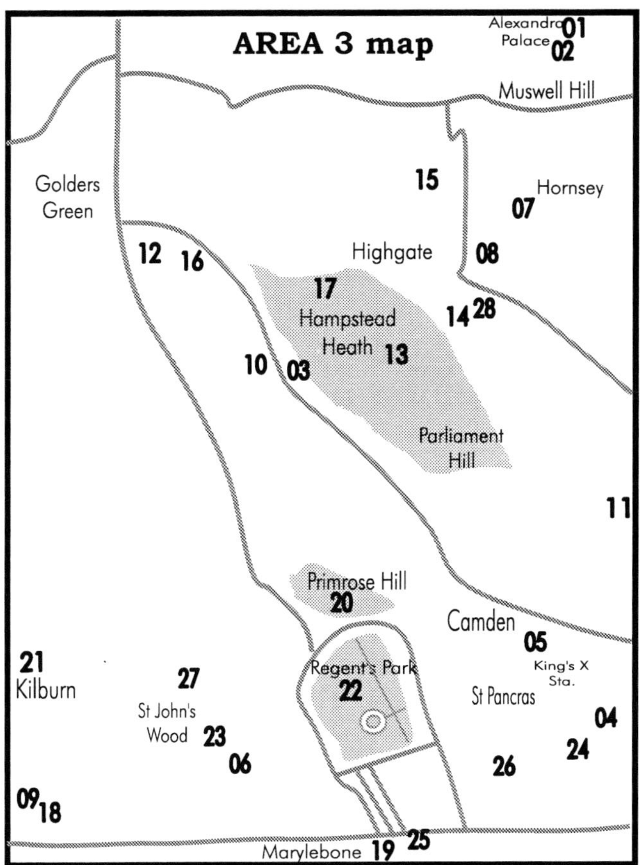
AREA 3 map
Alexandra Palace 01 02
Muswell Hill
15
Hornsey
07
Golders Green
Highgate
08
12
16
17
Hampstead Heath
13
14 28
10
03
Parliament Hill
11
Primrose Hill
20
Camden
05
21
Kilburn
27
Regent's Park
22
King's X Sta.
St Pancras
04
St John's Wood
23
06
26
24
09 18
Marylebone
19
25

AREA 3 - Alexandra Palace, Highgate, Hampstead, Regent's Park, Kilburn

01. ALEXANDRA PALACE

(Alexandra Palace Trust)

Grounds daily. Palm Court closed when used for events.

Alexandra Palace Way, Wood Green NE22 7AY Tel:0208 365 2671

This huge 'white elephant' dominates the north London skyline; and likewise the views from it are extensive. Palm trees tower up to the light in the glass-domed Palm Court. Outside, the 480 acres of parkland has much woodland planting, open grass areas and a nature reserve.

Café. Rail: Alexandra Palace Station

02. ALEXANDRA PALACE GARDEN CENTRE

(Capital Gardens PLC)

9am - 5pm mon - sat; 10.30am - 4.30pm sundays

Alexandra Palace N22 4BB Tel: 0208 444 2555

Part of the Capital Gardens chain of garden centres. Supplies a wide range of garden plants and sundries. Recently rebuilt and refurbished shop and café.

Café. Rail: Alexandra Palace Station

03. BURGH HOUSE

(Burgh House Trust)

wed - sun 12 - 5pm

New End Square, Hampstead NW3 1LT Tel: 0207 431 0144

Narrow country-style borders surround the pretty early 18th century house, now an art gallery and community centre. Gertrude Jekyll had a hand in some of the improvements to this small garden, and her influence can be seen in the paths inlaid with geometric patterns and in the continuing ethos of herbaceous and shrub planting.
Café. Tube: Hampstead

04. CALTHORPE PROJECT

Summer 10am - 6pm; Winter 9.30am - 5pm
258-274 Gray's Inn Road WC1 Tel: 0207 837 8019
A colourful and exuberent one acre garden set up by the local community to combat threat of development. A lot of the work done in the garden is paid for through fund-raising and is carried out by volunteers. A bridge from the entrance takes you over a lower garden and gives you a view of the roof garden, and leads you into a garden with mosaic on paths and in the walls, with rich and varied planting everywhere! A garden for all ages.
Plants for sale. Toilets/and for disabled. Under 8's play area. Over 8's adventure area. Train/Tube: Kings Cross

05. CAMLEY STREET NATURAL PARK

(Managed by London Wildlife Trust)
CLOSED Friday. Mon - Thurs 9am-5pm. W'end 11am-5pm
12 Camley Street NW1 Tel: 020 7833 2311
Community nature reserve thriving as a wonderful example of land use from industrial reclamation. The

two acre site slips between the Regent's Canal, with its lock and narrow boats, and the gasometers behind Kings Cross and St Pancras Stations. A path takes you around the site, through different habitats. These include a wildflower meadow, pondside areas with associated marsh, open water and reed bed habitats, and the light woodland which encloses the park. The Visitor Centre regularly runs activities for children, and has lots of information.

Toilets and for disabled. Train/tube: King's Cross. No dogs or cycles.

06. CLIFTON NURSERIES

8.30am - 5.30pm

5a Clifton Villas, Little Venice W2 9PH Tel: 0207 289 6851

¾ acre site crammed with plants. Specialising in topiary, statuary, specimen trees and shrubs for instant effect. Also unusual and exotic greenhouse and conservatory plants.

Tube: Warwick Avenue

07. CROUCH HILL FOREST GARDEN

(Naturewise)

daily

Crouch Hill Recreation Centre N8 3RX Tel: 020 7281 3765

"A forest garden is a sustainable edible landscape, designed to mirror the natural structure of woodlands, with their tree, shrub and herb associations." The Crouch Hill Forest Garden is a simple example, with different canopy layers on a slope behind a housing block.

08. ELTHORNE PARK
(London Borough of Islington)
daily 8am - dusk
Hazellville Road N19
Local park, with laurel-lined walkways and woodland areas.
Childrens playground. Train: Crouch Hill

ELTHORNE PARK - Noel Baker Peace Garden
A good example of a late 20th Century public garden. Small, well designed, formal space, with a strong range of landscape planting and a water feature.

09. EMSLIE HORNIMAN PLEASANCE
(The Royal Borough of Kensington and Chelsea)
daily
Bosworth Road, W10
An attractive and historically interesting five acre park that has recently had a major refurbishment. There is new landscaping and planting around the listed buildings and there is a 1920's garden.
Children's play areas.

10. FENTON HOUSE
(The National Trust)
March w'ends 2-5pm; April-Oct Wed-Fri 2-5pm; w'ends & Bank Hol Mons 11am-5pm.

Windmill Hill, Hampstead NW3 6RT Tel: 0207 435 3471

Fenton House was built in the 1690's, and is one of the oldest houses in Hampstead. The charming and well kept 1½ acre walled garden is in the country garden style, and was created to compliment the house. The garden is on three levels. There is a lawn area, sunken rose garden (recently replanted), scented garden, herbaceous borders, orchard and kitchen garden. Fenton House contains a rare collection of early keyboard instruments and porcelain.

Admission: Garden - free. House £4.30. About 1/3 of site is suitable for wheelchairs. WC only available if visiting house. Tube: Hampstead + 300m walk up Holly Hill. 'Phone for events, concerts etc.

11. FREIGHTLINERS CITY FARM

Tues - Sun 9am-5pm. Closed for lunch 1-2pm. CLOSED mondays

Sheringham Road N7 Tel: 020 7609 0467 Web: www.freightlinersfarm.org.uk

Chickens, pigs, goats and more, in variety create a cacophany of sound. Plants and gardens are not forgotten in this city farm environment, with a small ornamental garden on one side of the yard, and small kitchen garden on another. Fruit trees, herbs, ornamental shrubs and herbaceous plants thrive in raised beds - and are plentifully mulched from the endless resource nearby!

Good access for wheelchairs. Plants for sale. Train/ Tube: Highbury & Islington

12. GOLDERS HILL

(Corporation of London)

7.30 am - dusk. Greenhouse open weekends only, 2-4 pm

Hampstead Heath Tel: 0208 455 5183

36 acres of rolling parkland with good views out across London. The Café and flower garden are on the north side, menagerie at s.west. The 2 acre flower garden harks back to its Victorian roots, with vivid bedding and perennial plants. If you get the chance, visit the Glasshouse, open at weekends. The gentle woodland garden leads away from this area, and is pretty in spring, with rhododendrons and shade-loving plants.

Toilets & for disabled. Café. Tube: Golders Green

13. HAMPSTEAD HEATH

(Corporation of London)

daily

Hampstead Information Centre: Tel: 0207 482 7073

700 acres of open space with woodland, grassland and many ponds. The ancient woodland on the Heath is said to be a remnant of the Middlesex Forest. Many recreational facilities, from bathing in the famous bathing pools, some of which are natural, to kite flying. One of the peculiar bye-laws is that ladies may sunbathe topless, provided they do not stand up!

Toilets & for diasabled. Café. Tube: Hampstead

14. HIGHGATE CEMETERY

10am - 4pm

Swains Lane N6 Tel: 0208 340 1834

The maintenace regime in this, the most famous Victorian cemetery in the country, has meant that it has become like a 37 acre nature reserve. Memorials and tombstones emerge from the trees and grasses, and the area around the catacombs is most eerie. Many eminent Victorians were buried here. Please 'phone to check the cemetery is open - if there is a funeral, it will be closed to the public.

Tube: Highgate. Admission fees.

15. HIGHGATE WOOD

(Corporation of London)

Daily 7.30am - dusk

Intersection of Archway road and Muswell Hill, Highgate Tel: 0208 444 6129

70 acres. Originally part of Middlesex Forest, it is mainly oak, hornbeam and holly, with other self-sown trees and shrubs. This park has been awarded 'green Flag' Status.

Good access for wheelchairs; Toilets. Café. Award-winning childrens playground. Tube: Highgate

16. HILL GARDEN, THE

(Corporation of London)

Daily 9am - dusk

Iverforth Close, North End Way, Hampstead NW3

A wow! garden! Bold and brilliant landscape design from the Edwardian era, with rare and unusual plants; all brilliantly rescued and restored by the Corporation from a state of decay and dereliction. In 1904, Lord

Leverhulme commissioned the foresighted landscape architect Thomas Mawson to design his hillside garden with a brief for it to be good for entertaining, whilst screening it from passers by on surrounding Hampstead Heath. The final result (after additions and amendments), is an 800 feet long 'L'-shaped pergola, at ground level near the house, and 30 feet above it where the hillside drops away at the far end. Smooth, white doric columns, of Portland stone bear oak beams, around and along which climbers twine - there must have been some amazing parties here! The west end of the pergola juts above a terrace garden, with formal rectangular pool and gazebo. Just go and see it!

Partial access for wheelchairs. Tube: Golders Green

The Hill Garden

17. KENWOOD HOUSE

(English Heritage)

8am - dusk

Hampstead Lane, Hampstead NW3 Tel: 0208 348 1286

The pristine cream-coloured neo-classical mansion, remodelled by Robert Adam in 1764, stands above lawns that sweep down to an ornamental lake. Humphrey Repton laid out the design for these grounds in 1793. Mature 'Hankerchief Tree's' (Davidia involucrata), 'Swamp Cypress' (Taxodium distichum) and 'Chinese Elm (Zelkova) tree species may be found and the rhododendrons and azaleas make a bright display in May.

Toilets / and for disabled. Café. Tube: Highgate + 15mins walk or 210 bus

18. MEANWHILE GARDENS

Daily

156 - 158 Kensal Road W10 5BN Tel/Fax: 0208 960 4600

4 acre community garden reclaimed from derelict land in 1977. Designed by a sculptor, the site has been transformed with slopes and paths winding through trees, shrubberies, a wildlife garden and a large pond. The soil varies over the site from heavy clay to light and rubbly. Mediterranean plants are grown in the dry and hot areas. There is a large spring flowering ceanothus, and the caryopteris are wonderful in the autumn. The garden has recently undergone a major

refurbishment, with extensive new planting and walkways.

Supervised Under 5's children's playground. Tube: Westbourne Park

19. PADDINGTON STREET GARDENS

(City of Westminster)

daily 10am - dusk

Paddington St W1

Pleasant and well kept gardens just off Marylebone High Street. Most of the buildings around this 2 ½ acre park back on to it, rather than face it, as it was originally a burial ground. It is in fact still consecrated, but there are few references to this - a small mausoleum, which now incongruously has hanging baskets attached to it. There is a good children's playground and two pavilions - and if you need to use the toilet, the nearby Paddington Street public toilets have won the City of Westminster 'Loo of the Year' awards! Therein you can be soothed with muzac and there are murals, not graffitti on the walls.

Toilets/ and for disabled; children's play area

20. PRIMROSE HILL

(Royal Parks Agency)

daily

Prince Albert Road NW1

50 acres of grass and parkland trees with wonderful views, which is divided from Regent's Park by the busy Prince Albert Road. The viewpoint is 219ft above sea level, and many famous landmarks can be seen from

it, including St. Paul's Cathedral, the Houses of Parliament, Centre Point and the Telecom Tower.
Children's playground. Toilets.

21. QUEEN'S PARK

(Corporation of London)
daily
Kilburn
30 acres of parkland and ornamental gardens. This park has been awarded 'Green Flag' status.
Children's playground and paddling pool.

22. REGENT'S PARK

(Royal Parks Agency)
daily 5am - dusk
NW1
Famous park on the north edge of central London. The part-built idea for a grand garden suburb, designed by John Nash (1752 - 1835), architect to the Crown, for the Prince Regent, later to become George IV. What was built, and still survives, are all recognisable as a part of one dream, where creamy-pink stucco Regency houses face elegant park and gardens. The whole lot is now Grade I listed, down to the last lamp-post & bollard.

Regent's Park - AVENUE GARDENS

A pair of formal gardens sweep half way up the Broad Walk. Italianate in style, immaculate with fountains, shallow urns known as 'Tazza's' and clever ideas for bedding out. These gardens were laid out in 1864 to a design by William Nesfield, a prominent Victorian garden designer. However, over time the gardens had deteriorated and in 1993/4 were wonderfully restored as a prime example of their kind and are award-winningly maintained.

Regent's Park - QUEEN MARY'S GARDENS

A series of gardens within the Inner Circle, including Queen Mary's Rose Garden, a Fossil Garden, the Sunken or Begonia Garden, a Woodland Garden, Rock Garden, pond, waterfall, cascade and more. The Rose garden is a large area encircled by rose - festooned rope swags. This stands at the head of a series of rose gardens, in all growing around 30,000 roses - the colour and scent a feast for the senses. Beyond these lie the pond, cascade, rock garden and fossil garden. The sunken garden has a formal layout of bedding, secluded by a clipped yew hedge. There are many mature specimen trees, such as Swamp Cypress (Taxodium distichum) and Manna Ash (Fraxinus ornus), and a wide variety shrubs and hebaceous plants; the herbaceous borders are particularly well stocked. Despite its age, and many years of establishment, the garden feels alive and vibrant, with areas being rejuvenated and immaculately kept as necessary.

Regent's Park - ST JOHN'S LODGE

Inner Circle Road

Elegant town garden overlooked but divided off from the handsome building of St John's Lodge, designed by Decimus Burton as part of Nash's plan. A wide passage interspersed with several metal pergola hoops leads down to the main garden. Here herbaceous borders edged with lavender lead to a series of three circular gardens, each enclosed by pleached lime.

23. REMBRANDT GARDENS

(City of Westminster)
daily
Warwick Avenue W9
Pretty garden area of 1½ acres near the canal in the Little Venice area. When seen in the summer, it was overspilling with roses, HT's and shrub roses in the borders and climbing and rambling roses on the walls.
Tube: Warwick Avenue

24. ST GEORGE'S GARDENS

(London Borough of Camden)
daily, daylight hours
Heathcote Street WC1
In this quiet oasis of mature trees and pretty shrub borders, there are many statues and memorials which make reference to the original use of these gardens - a burial ground, the first in London not to be sited next to its church. The site has had extensive infrastructure restoration and refurbishment with the path network restored to its original layout, new planting areas, and

restored tombstones and chapel (not open to the public).
Tube: Russell Square

25. ST MARYLEBONE PARISH CHURCH GROUNDS

(City of Westminster)
daily
Marylebone Road NW1
Plain, quiet church grounds of ½ an acre, dominated by the church and a huge plane tree. Grass, clipped hedges and shrub borders

26. TAVISTOCK SQUARE

(London Borough of Camden)
8am - dusk
WC1
A London square that has nearly become a 'Peace Garden' with the many commemorative trees and artefacts, especially the statue of Ghandi in the centre. Pollarded limes line the perimeter path. Rose borders and seasonal bedding add colour to the centre - the heavy perfume from a bed of polyanthus could be detected 100 yards away in the spring.

27. VIOLET HILL GARDENS

(City of Westminster)
daily
NW8
A 'Jewel' of a garden, with lawns, mature trees and shrubs including a huge tulip tree (Liriodendron tulipifera).

Children's play area.

28. WATERLOW PARK
(London Borough of Camden)
daily
Highgate High Street N19
26 hillside acres set between Highgate Cemetery and the High Street. A mature park bequethed by its then owner Sir Sydney Waterlow as 'a garden for the gardenless'. Hence mature trees and shrub borders, rose beds and a rock garden. There are large ponds on three levels, providing habitat for a variety of wildfowl. There is also an aviary at the bottom of the park. The terrace gardens around Lauderdale House are due to be restored, as are other areas within the site.
Café. Toilets. Children's play area

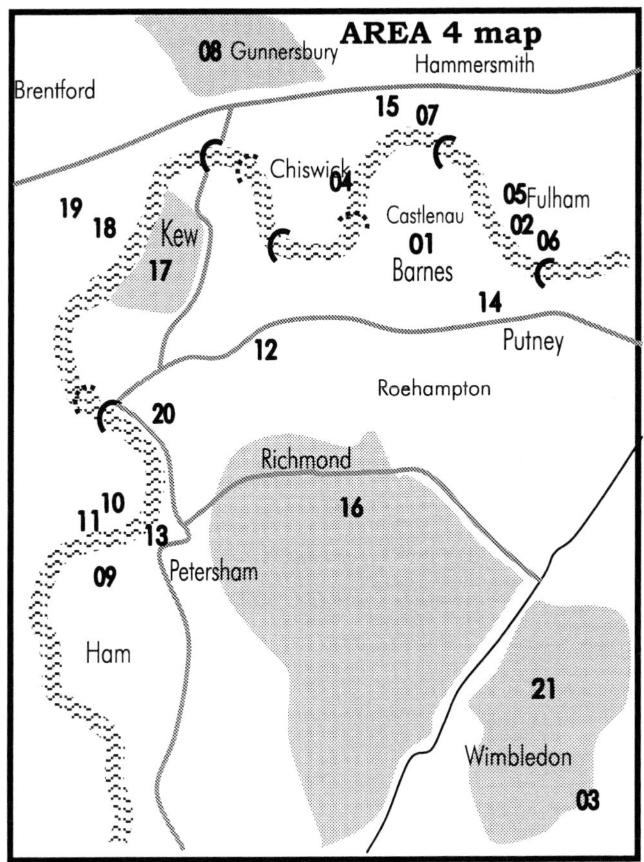
AREA 4 map
08 Gunnersbury
Hammersmith
Brentford
15
07
Chiswick
04
05 Fulham
19
18
Kew
Castlenau
02
06
01
17
Barnes
14
Putney
12
Roehampton
20
Richmond
10
11
16
13
09
Petersham
Ham
21
Wimbledon
03

AREA 4 - Fulham, Wimbledon, Richmond, Kew, Chiswick, Hammersmith

01. BARNES COMMON

daily

SW13

Large area of common land dissected by roads. The scrub and trees, such as birch, pine , oak and understory of gorse and broom make it a piece of wild land close to the heart of London.

02. BISHOP'S PARK

(London Borough of Hammersmith and Fulham)

8am - dusk

Bishop's Park Road, Fulham Tel: 0208 748 3020

Thames-side park with boating lake, paddling pool and aviary. Steps down from Putney Bridge take you into the Park, and you can walk from here to Hammersmith Bridge, through the Park and along the river. Trees, shrubs and seasonal bedding plants brighten the way. You also pass the small 'Rowberry Mead' with its wildflower area and chidren's play area.

Toilets & for disabled; Café. Children's play areas

03. CANNIZARO PARK

(London Borough of Merton)

mon - fri 8am - dusk; sat/sun 9am - dusk

Cannizaro Road, Wimbledon SW19 Tel: 0208 946 7349

Over 400 species of trees and shrubs set in what were the grounds of Cannizaro House (now a conference venue), on the edge of Wimbledon Common. The azalea dell is a blaze of colour throughout the spring. With a rose garden, fragrant in the summer and with such a variety of ornamental trees (cork oaks, sassafras, mulberries etc), this a garden to visit at any time of the year. New projects are ongoing, with the former heather garden to be transformed into a 'Mediterranean garden' and there is a developing 'azalea tunnel' in Lady Jane's wood. A modern scuplture/ fountain to mark the Millenium is in the middle of the front drive.
Toilets. Picnic area. Train/Tube: Wimbledon + 10 mins walk

04. CHISWICK HOUSE
(London Borough of Hounslow & English Heritage)
8.30am - dusk
Burlington Lane W4 2RP Tel: 0208 995 0508
Extensive 18th century gardens designed by William Kent in the Classical Style, to reflect Lord Burlington's newly built Palladian villa. Much of Kent's original design remains. Allées and vistas, a Ha-Ha (a design feature possibly invented by Kent), an amphitheatre and a long, canal-like lake with a cascade at one end. These features, with the many artefacts which dress the site, all contribute to the theatre of Kent's classical landscape. There is also a large camellia-filled Conservatory, built in 1813. Mature and specimen trees are throughout the site.

Refreshments (seasonal). Train: Chiswick + 10 mins walk. Tube: Turnham Green + 15 mins walk

05. FULHAM PALACE GARDEN CENTRE

(Fairbridge Charity)

mon - sat 9.30am - 5.30pm; 10am - 5pm sundays

Bishops Avenue SW6 6EE Tel: 0207 736 2640

Everything for the town gardener, specimen plants, roses, orchids, houseplants, trellis, window boxes and garden furniture. Not a very large site, but with an unusual glass-roofed building housing the shop, houseplants and garden sundries. This was built in 1984 with help from some of the youngsters involved with Fairbridge, a charity which helps young people in the inner city. Profits from the garden centre go to the charity.

Tube: Putney Bridge + 10 mins walk

06. FULHAM PALACE GARDENS

(London Borough of Hammersmith and Fulham)

8am - dusk; closed 25th Dec & 1st Jan

Bishops Avenue SW6 Tel: 0207 736 5821

Famous in the C17th, these are now Romantic gardens in the best tradition of Beauty and Decay. The 100+ yrs old wisteria that envelops the trellis in the walled garden is not to be missed in May. If you can ignore the air of neglect, there are some fine and unusual plants to be seen here.

Braille board in walled garden. Childrens play area. Tube: Putney Bridge + 10 mins walk through Bishops Park.

Wisteria Trellis, Kitchen Garden, Fulham Palace

07. FURNIVAL GARDENS

(London Borough of Hammersmith & Fulham)

daily

Great West Road, Hammersmith W6

Charming gardens next to the river. Part of the Thames Walk, there are views down to Hammersmith Bridge.

Tube: Ravenscourt Park

08. GUNNERSBURY PARK

(London Borough of Hounslow & Ealing)

daily 8am - dusk

Popes Lane W3 8LQ Tel: 020 8993 2055

18th Century landscape of historic importance, currently undergoing some much needed restoration. If you have a morning to peruse the 186 acres, there are many features to see: a doric-style temple, an orangery, the neo-classical 'Large Mansion' (now the museum), Princess Amelia's Bath House, a gothic tower and 'Potomac Fishing Pond'.

There are many fine trees in the park, approximately 150 different species, over 2000 trees in total, 'Tulip Trees', Cedars, Redwoods and 'Indian Bean Tree' to name but a few. The Museum is open from 1pm, and is the former home of the Rothschilds, whose ownership was the most significant influence at Gunnersbury. Much of the interior from their time is still to be seen, with grand state apartments, the 'Long Gallery' and Victorian kitchens.

Café. Toilets & for disabled; Picnic areas. Children's play areas. Tube: Acton Town

09. HAM HOUSE

(National Trust)

April - October Sat - Weds 10.30am - dusk

Ham Street, Ham, Richmond TW10 7RS Tel: 0208 940 1950

18 acres of 17th century formal gardens undergoing restoration, surrounding the pretty Ham House . A formal Knot Garden, of low hedges punctuated by clipped box cones and infilled with lavender and santolina, is surrounded by a cloister of pleached hornbeam and gravel paths. There is a fine example of a 'Wilderness', a 17th Century idea for the garden, and much more structured than present day

interpretation. The Orangery, also 17th century, is one of the earliest surviving examples in the country. The grounds are full of interesting and unusual plants.
Admission to grounds £2. Toilets/and for disabled. Café. Guide Dogs only. Train: Richmond

10. MARBLE HILL HOUSE
(English Heritage)
7.30am - dusk
Richmond Road, Twickenham TW1 2NL Tel: 0208 892 5115
This small Palladian villa sits like a doll's house in the surrounding simple 18th century landscape. It was built in 1724-9 for Henrietta Howard, mistress of George II. She had much help and advice with the garden from contempories such as Alexander Pope (who lived just along the river at Strawberry Hill) Horace Walpole and Charles Bridgeman. There is a grotto, an ice house and some mature and historic trees, including a massive Black Walnut (Juglans nigra) which was planted during Henrietta's lifetime. The double avenue of horse chestnut trees is at its best when flowering in May. The views from the lawns in front of the house would originally have cast south to the river, but this is now mostly obscured.
Café (seasonal). Train: St. Margaret's or Twickenham

11. ORLEANS HOUSE GALLERY GARDEN
(London Borough of Richmond upon Thames)
daily 9am - sunset

Riverside, Twickenham, Middlesex TW1 3DJ Tel: 020 8892 0221

The remaining buildings of Orleans House (which is now a Gallery) are two wings and the pretty 18th century Octagon Room. They are surrounded by a woodland garden, which overlooks the Thames. A large Catalpa bignoniodes (Indian Bean Tree) stands in front of the buildings.

Train: Twickenham or St. Margaret's.

12. PALM CENTRE, THE

daily 10am - 6pm or dusk if earlier.

Ham Central Nursery, Ham Street, Ham, Richmond TW10 7HA Tel: 0208 255 6191

Large nursery in south west London. Built up over the past ten years, the nursery's speciality of palms has increased with the inclusion of bamboos, cycads, tree ferns and bananas. Other exotic plants are sold here too.

Tube: Stockwell

13. PETERSHAM NURSERIES

mon - sat 9am - 5.30pm; sun 10am - 4pm. Closed Christmas, Boxing & New Year's days.

Petersham Road, Petersham, Richmond TW10 7AG Tel: 0208 940 5230

A large site tucked away down a little road leading on to meadowland near the Thames and not far from Richmond Park. There are several large greenhouses, some with young plants being grown on, and another housing the shop and frost tender plants. This nursery

grows 99% of the spring bedding it sells. Ornamental and fruit trees, roses, climbers, shrubs and herbaceous plants, as well as seasonal bedding and garden sundries are all to be found at this nursery garden.
Toilets.

14. PUTNEY GARDEN CENTRE
(Adrian Hall)
mon - sat 9am - 5.30pm; sun & bank hols 10am - 4pm
Dryburgh Road, Putney SW15 1BN Tel: 0208 789 9518
This garden centre is tucked below the road and the railway line, and as you travel along Dyburgh Road, you look down onto the mass of blooms below. The centre stocks a wide range of plants and garden sundries, including pots, paving, containers and trellis.
Toilets. Train: Barnes

15. RAVENSCOURT PARK
(London Borough of Hammersmith & Fulham)
daily
Ravenscourt Road W6
Attractive medium-sized public park. There is a scented garden, nature area, lake, shrubberies and seasonal bedding and large areas of grass.
Children's play areas; Café; Toilets; Tube: Ravenscourt Park

16. RICHMOND PARK
(Royal Parks Agency)
7.30am - dusk

Tel: 0208 948 3209

At nearly 2,500 acres, this is the largest park in London spreading along flat lands on an east bank of the River Thames. Open sweeps of grass and heathland are broken up by ponds, lakes and ancient trees, mainly oak and are grazed by herds of deer, 400 fallow and 200 red at any one time. There are also several woods, the prettiest of which is the Isabella Plantation. This 40 acre woodland garden is full of rhododendrons, camellias and magnolias, and carpeted with daffodills, then bluebells in the spring. Herbaceous plants grow on the banks of the streams, and fothergillas, euonymus (the native Spindle Tree) ornamental birch, maple and cherry contribute to the autumn display, as does the Acer Glade. Other horticultural delights to be found in the Park include the Formal gardens and Laburnum Walk at Pembroke House, and the Rose Garden at King Henry VIII's mound.

Café. Toilets

17. ROYAL BOTANIC GARDENS KEW

(The Trustees)

Daily 9.30am to variable evening closing. Closed 25 Dec & 1st Jan

Kew, Richmond, Surrey TW9 3AB Tel: 0208 332 5655 Web: www.kew.org.

Kew, which is primarily a research institute, is one of the main centres of botanical study in the world. 300 acres of internationally renown gardens. Numerous gardens devoted to specific plant types, many garden features including four magnificent acres of glasshouses, the Pagoda, acres of rare and historic trees...there is too much to describe, and always plenty to see.

Admission: Adults £5; Concessions £3.50; Children (5-16) £2.50; Family ticket £13. Toilets and for the disabled. Café. Gift shop. Tube/ Train: Kew Gardens. Train: Kew Bridge

18. SYON HOUSE & PARK

(The Duke of Northumberland)

10am - 5.30pm or dusk if earlier. Closed 25 & 26 Dec.

Syon Park, Brentford, Middlesex TW8 8JF Tel: 0208 560 0881

30 acres of gardens and 'Capability' Brown landscape form what is one of the oldest landscaped sites in the country, and has been owned by the Percy family since 1594. The gardens contain over 200 diverse tree species, a long lake and the beautiful Great Conservatory. Restoration and improvements are ongoing including reopening the view across the Thames to Kew.

Café. Toilets. Train/Tube: Kew Bridge or Gunnersby + 237 or 267 bus to Brent Lea.

19. SYON PARK GARDEN CENTRE

(Wyvale Garden Centres PLC)

mon - sat 9am - 5.30pm; sun 10.30am - 4.30pm. Closed 25 & 26 December

Wyevale Garden Centre Syon Park, Syon Park, Brentford, Middlesex TW8 8JG Tel: 0208 568 0134

Large retail garden centre with a wide range of plants.

20. TERRACE GARDENS

(London Borough of Richmond upon Thames)
daily 7.30am - dusk
Petersham Road, Richmond
Well kept gardens steeply rising from Petersham Road up to Richmond Hill. There is an underground passage from these gardens through to the riverside park. The passage comes out into a flint encrusted grotto facing the Thames. The formal areas of the Terrace gardens have lawns and seasonal bedding. Surrounding is informal woodland planting with shade loving shrubs and herbaceous plants growing under the canopy of trees. Amelanchier, spiraea and prunus were looking good when seen in the spring. A rare Coate-Stone statue of the river god 'Thames' faces the Petersham Road entrance. There is also a large rustic thatched summer-house and a conservatory which although not often open, allows an easy view in to the tender plants growing inside.
Toilets in riverside park.

21. WIMBLEDON COMMON

(London Borough of Merton)
daily
Wimbledon
460 acres of open grass, trees, woodland, birch & heather heath. Watch out for the Wombles...

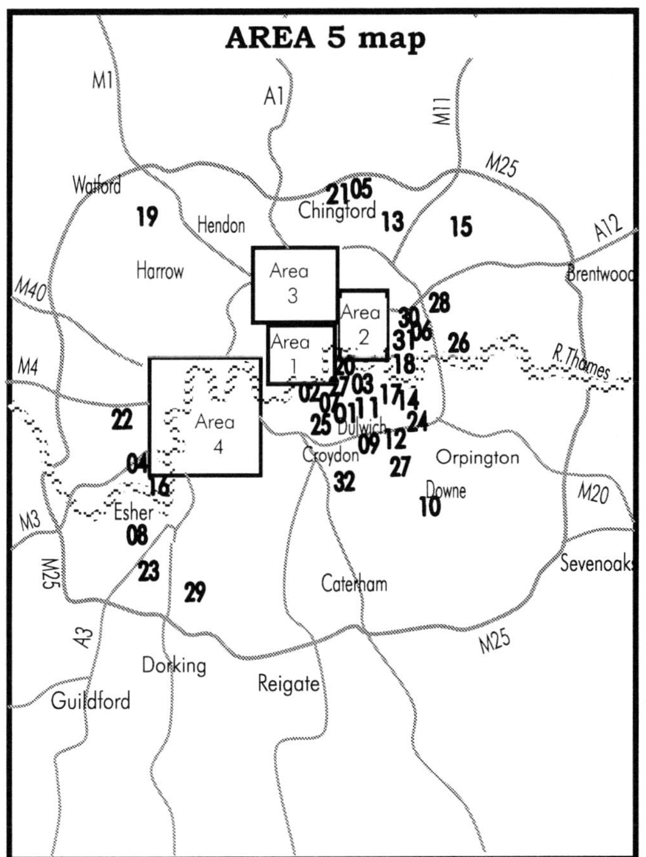
AREA 5 map
M1
A1
M11
M25
Watford
19
Hendon
2105
Chingford
13
15
A12
Harrow
Area 3
Area 2
Area 1
Area 4
Brentwood
M40
28
30
31
06
26
R.Thames
M4
20
18
02
27
03
17
14
07
01
11
22
25
Dulwich
24
09
12
Croydon
Orpington
04
27
16
32
Downe
10
M20
Esher
M3
08
23
29
M25
Caterham
Sevenoaks
A3
M25
Dorking
Reigate
Guildford

AREA 5 - Outer London

01. BELAIR PARK

(London Borough of Southwark)
daily 8am - dusk
Gallery Road, Dulwich Tel: 020 8693 5737
This 10ha park was originally laid out to compliment Belair Mansion (now a restaurant) and has been awarded a Grade II listing. It is an informal, sloping site, sweeping down with ancient trees, shrubberies and rose beds to a long meandering lake.
Train: West Dulwich.

02. BROCKWELL PARK

(London Borough of Lambeth)
daily
Herne Hill, Norwood Road SE24
Large Park - 128 acres. The secret walled garden is ordered and tranquil, with herbaceous plants and mature yew hedges. There is also a C19th clock tower, ornamental pond, picnic area and there are 1¾ miles of cycle paths. Many community activities take place in this park.
Café; Toilets; Children's play areas. Train: Herne Hill

03. BURGESS PARK

(London Borough of Southwark)
daily 9am - 5pm
Albany Road SE5 Tel: 020 7525 1050
Created from the 1960's, the landscaping involves 55ha of walking and recreational areas. There are

formal gardens, wildlife areas, copses and meadows, sports pitches and a fishing lake.
Good access for wheelchairs. Toilets/ and for disabled. Tube: Elephant & Castle

Burgess Park - CHUMLEIGH MULTICULTURAL GARDEN
daily 10am - 5pm or dusk if earlier.
Burgess Park SE5 Tel: 0207 525 1050
Chumleigh Gardens is a one acre walled garden within Burgess Park, created around the 1820's Almshouses. The walls provide an ideal micoclimate to grow plants from all over the world in thc 'Multicultural Gardens'. These gardens each reflect a cultural identity from thc country of origin. The Garden representations are: English; Oriental; Afri-Caribbean; Islamic and Meditteranean. Plants that can be found include: Umbrella or Stone Pine (Pinus pinea); Loquat (Eriobotrya japonica), tree fern and Albizzia julibrissin with its pink fluffy flowers in summer.
Good access for wheelchair users. Toilets/ and for disabled. Café (seasonal). Tube: Elephant & Castle.

04. BUSHY PARK
(Royal Parks Agency)
daily
Hampton Court Road, Hampton Hill TW12 2EJ Tel: 0208 979 1586
Over 1000 acres of rural parkland on the north side of Hampton Court. Natural - style gardens can be found on the site, the largest being the Waterhouse

Woodland Gardens. Here rhododendrons and azaleas bloom in May, and woodland herbaceous plants display as well. Camellias are wonderful in late winter/early spring. There is also a 'Scented Glade' filled with the perfume from the yellow-flowered Azalea lutea, a 'Bog Garden' with Gunnera, skunk cabbage (not so pleasantly perfumed), hostas, candelabra primulas and rodgersias, a 'Wild Garden', heather beds and a fritillary meadow. Canadian plants surround a Totem pole in the 'Canadian Glade'. The 17th century Diana fountain is a reference point on the majestic Chestnut Avenue.
Rail: Teddington; Hampton Wick

05. CAPEL MANOR GARDENS

(Capel Manor Charitable Organisation)
Open: April - September weekdays 10am - 5.30pm, weekends 11am - 6pm; March & October CLOSED Saturdays. Nov - Feb weekdays ONLY.
Bullsmoor Lane, Enfield, Middlesex EN1 4RQ Tel: 0208 366 4442
30 acres of gardens, now part of the horticultural college at Capel Manor (plant labelling is good!). There are many 'Theme Gardens', a Japanese Garden, an Italianate Maze, an Allergenic garden, a sensory garden, a garden designed for wheelchair users, and a garden dedicated to the memory of Diana, Princess of Wales. The College has National Collections of Achillea and of Sarcococca.
Admission: Adults £4; Concessions £3.50; Children(3-16yrs) £2; Family £10. Nov-Feb cheaper winter rates apply. Free

wheelchair loan (please book), and free entry for wheelchair assistants. Refreshments. Toilets/ and for disabled. Rail: Turkey Street.

06. CITY OF LONDON CEMETERY - CEMETERY TREE TRAIL

(Corporation of London)

9am - dusk

City of London Cemetery, East London Tel: 0208 530 2151

Treemendous! Wonderful trees from all over the world may be found throughout this huge Victorian cemetery, and make up one of the largest tree trails in Europe. Wingnuts and cedars, cypress and maples jostle for position amongst the massive memorials. Avenues lined with trees, rhododendrons and other shrubs link each section of the site. Trees that may be found include the 'Incense Cedar' (Calocedrus decurrens), 'Pere David's Maple' (Acer davidii), 'Californian Redwood' (Sequoia sempervirens) and the pink-flowered 'Indian Horse Chestnut' (Aesculus indica).

Train: Manor Park

07. CLAPHAM COMMON

(London Borough of Lambeth)

daily

Windmill Drive SW4

190 acres. Roughly triangular, dissected by some roads. Large open grass areas with many trees, three ornamental ponds, bandstand, refreshment facilities

and a paddling pool. Many community events take place here.
Tube: Clapham Common

08. CLAREMONT LANDSCAPE GARDEN

(The National Trust)
Daily 10am - 5pm. Closed Mondays Nov - March, also 25 Dec & 1 Jan
Portsmouth Road, Esher Surrey KT10 9JG. Tel: 01372 467 806.
18th Century landscape gardens with, amongst others, William Kent and 'Capability' Brown involved in its construction. The most famous feature is the turf amphitheatre. There is also a lake with a grotto on one side, an island with a recently restored pavilion, belvedere, camellia terrace and some good viewpoints and vistas.
Admission: Adults £3.50; Children £1.75; Family ticket £7.50. Braille guide available. 2 wheelchairs available - please book. Toilets & for disabled. Café.

09. CRYSTAL PALACE PARK

(London Borough of Bromley)
7.30am - dusk
Thicket Road SE20 Tel: 0208 778 9496
200 acre park designed and landscaped by Joseph Paxton to re-house his magnificent Crystal Palace from the Great Exhibition site in Hyde Park in 1851. Unfortunately the massive and intricate glasshouse was destroyed by fire in 1936 and only the site of its foundations remain. What is of most fun however, is

the Dinosaur Park, built in 1854 (a kind of Victorian 'Jurassic Park'). Remarkably, 29 of the original, life-size monsters remain. There is also a lake, a maze and plenty of parkland trees. Please note that the park is undergoing extensive refurbishment, and some areas will be closed until 2002 - 'phone for details.
Toilets/ and for disabled. Café. Train: Crystal Palace

10. DOWN HOUSE

(English Heritage)
Weds - Sun 10am - 5pm. Closed 24 - 26 Dec & 1 - 28 Feb.
Luxted Road, Downe Tel: 01689 859 119. Booking Line: 0870 603 0145
Charles Darwin's 18 acre estate, largely unaltered since his death in 1882. The gardens surround the house, and he developed both as places to test his research and ideas. Garden features include the 'Sand Walk' or 'thinking path' around the wood he planted, which is full of bluebells and anenomes in the spring; orchard; greenhouses, containing orchids and carnivorous plants, both of which he used in his studies of plant growth; the flower garden directly outside the house; and the lawn, which contains rare grassland fungi.
Admission: BY PRE-BOOKED TICKET (at least 24hrs in advance) Adults: £5.50; Concessions: £4.10; Children: £2.80. Admission price includes entry to the house and guided tours. Café. Toilets and for disabled. Train: Orpington; Bromley South.

11. DULWICH PARK

(Southwark Borough Council)

daily 8am - dusk

College Road, Dulwich SE21 7QB Tel: 020 8693 5737

Although this 72 acre park was started in 1890 with land given by Dulwich College, it has a less formal layout than some Victorian parks. Features include the 'Japanese' Garden', the 'American Garden' which is ablaze with rhododendrons and azaleas in May, the boating lake, which has a Barbara Hepworth sculpture at one side and a newly created 'drought-tolerant' garden.

Café. Toilets & for disabled. Train: North Dulwich + 10mins walk

12. DULWICH UPPER WOOD NATURE PARK

Mon - Fri 10am - 5pm staffed; the wood is open daily

Farquhar Road, Crystal Palace SE19 1SS Tel: 0208 761 6230

This 5 acre wood is a remnant of the Great North Wood, and is one of the few sites of Ancient Woodland left within an urban environment. In the site there is a line of ancient coppiced trees which is an old woodland boundary, and a ditch which marks the sub-divisions of the Great North Wood. The wood is mixed oak and other native species, some of the oak trees being 400 years old. The site is used by local schools and colleges, and is managed as a nature reserve. There is a pond/ marsh area, made using the underlying London clay and a herb garden. A fern garden and a

fungi garden are planned. There are many wild plants and flowers to be seen, with carpets of bluebells, primroses and wood anenomes in the spring.
Train: Gipsy Hill.

13. EPPING FOREST

(Corporation of London)
Epping Forest Information Centre, High Beech, Loughton, Essex IG10 4AF: Tel: 020 8508 0028
At 19km long, and nearly 4km wide, Epping Forest was saved for public use from encroaching development in the late 19th century by the Corporation of London. The largest public space near London, 2/3 is SSSI, and 2/3 wooded. It provides wildlife habitat and conservation, as well as being used for sports such as golf, cricket, cross-country running and there is over 85km of track for horses. Conservation work includes re-cutting old pollards, pond and heathland restoration.

14. GREENWICH PARK

(Royal Parks Agency)
Dawn - dusk
SE10 Tel: 0208 858 2608
180 historic acres of open hillside and woodland criss-crossed by formal paths and avenues in a design by Andre le Notre (who laid out the garden at Versailles) make up this, the oldest enclosed Royal Park. The site slopes up, away from the Thames, to 150 feet at its highest point, behind the Royal Naval College

(designed by Sir Christopher Wren) and the Queen's House (designed by Inigo Jones in 1616). There is a herb garden by St. Mary's Lodge, down towards the Queen's House; a lake in the large Victorian Flower Garden, which is towards the southern edge of the site. This Flower Garden is colourful in the spring with azaleas, bulbs and rhododendrons; in the summer with herbaceous plants and dahlias; and in the autumn with colour from specimen trees such as the 'Tulip Tree' (Liriodendron), 'Maidenhair Tree' (Ginkgo biloba) and ornamental birch. Mature specimen conifers, such as of cypress, pine and cedar, and the heather beds, give all year round interest.
Café. Children's playground. Train: Greenwich.

15. HAINAULT FOREST COUNTRY PARK
(London Borough of Redbridge)
daily 7.30am - dusk
Romford Road, Chigwell, Essex IG7 4QN Tel: 020 8500 7353
600 acres of forest, wild flower meadows and grassland, with wonderful views over the London cityscape. Paths and tracks for horses, cycles and pedestrians lead throughout. There is a fishing lake and rare breeds farm.
Visitor Centre. Toilets. Refreshments. Picnic area. Tube: Hainault

16. HAMPTON COURT PALACE
(Historic Royal Palaces Agency)
Dawn - dusk

East Molesey, Surrey KT8 9AU Tel: 0208 781 9500
Extensive gardens surround this historic Royal Palace built in 1514. Many garden features, compiled throughout the centuries include: the famous and identifying vista of the Palace, through the Fountain Garden from the 'Long Water'; the award-winning restoration of the Privy Garden, a formal parterre laid out originally in the time of William III; a walled garden with extensively planted herbaceous beds; a 17th Century 'Wilderness'; and the (in)famous Maze ("Help Me! I'm Lost!" can be recognised in any language!). 70 acres of gardens in all. The Great Vine, planted in 1768 during 'Capability' Brown's tenure as Master Gardener still bears fruit prolifically. RHS show held here annually in July.
Admission: Grounds free except: Privy Garden, Sunken Garden & Great Vine £2; Maze: Adults £2; Children £1.20. Toilets. Restaurant. Much of interest to children. Train: Hampton Court.

17. HORNIMAN GARDENS

(Horniman Museum)
8am - dusk. Closed 25 Dec.
Hornimans Drive SE23 3BT Tel: 0208 699 8924
In the 1890's, Frederick Horniman, a wealthy Tea Merchant and collector, opened his collection to the public, for "those who use their eyes obtain the most enjoyment and knowledge; those who look but do not see go away no wiser than when they came." The museum is housed in a beautiful Art-Nouveau building and contains a wide range of anthropological items. The gardens are alongside the museum. There is an

unusual, recently rebuilt Victorian conservatory which is intricately patterned with ironwork and glass; elsewhere, the gardens have nature trails, an animal enclosure and plenty of grass for children to run about on. The best views out are across west London, to the North Downs and are from the Rose garden and Sunken garden. It must be noted that the museum is currently undergoing extensive refurbishment, with some of the galleries closed until 2002. If you are wishing to see a specific item, please 'phone first. The gardens remain open.
Toilets/ and for disabled. Train: Forest Hill

18. ISLAND GARDENS

(London Borough of Tower Hamlets)
daily
E14
Plain but pretty gardens on the north bank of the Thames, with plane trees, grass and seasonal bedding. What makes these gardens particularly interesting, though are their links with Greenwich, directly across the river. For one, there is the Greenwich foot tunnel, running under the Thames from these gardens to the Cutty Sark on the south side. The views across to Greenwich from these gardens are all the painted views of Wren's masterpiece of perspective, order and design - really one of London's sights.
Toilets. Refreshments. Train: DLR - Island Gardens

19. JACQUES AMAND INTERNATIONAL

Mon - Sat 10am-4pm. Closed Saturdays in January.

Seasonally open on Sundays.
The Nurseries, 146 Clamp Hill, Stanmore HA7 Tel: 0208 420 7110.
Specialist grower of bulb and woodland plants. Retails from nursery and shop. (The shop is run by the SHAW trust). Catalogue and mail-order service available. If you wish to visit the nursery, or are looking for a specific plant, please 'phone first.

20. KENNINGTON PARK

(London Borough of Lambeth)
daily
St. Agnes Place SE11
36 acres of open grass areas, and tree lined walks. There is a charming flower garden at one end, with a pergola dripping with wisteria when seen in May. The small sunken area as you enter this flower garden, the crazy paving and surrounding herbaceous borders all combine to leave an impression of an Arts and Crafts influence. The rest of the park has mature trees, large areas of grass and sports pitches. Many local community events take place here.
Toilets & for disabled. Children's play areas; Tube: Oval

21. MYDDLETON HOUSE

(Lee Valley Regional Park Authority)
Mon - Fri 10am - 4pm, and last sundays of Feb & March (bulbs). Also from Easter - October on Sundays, Bank Holidays and on National Gardens Scheme days 2pm - 5pm . Closed Christmas week.

Bulls Cross Lane, Enfield Tel: 01992 702 200
Created by E.A. Bowles (1865 - 1954), famous plantsman, botanist, author and artist. Informal, natural gardens with something of interest all year round. A dry, free-draining soil means that bulbs naturalise easily, and the drive up to the house is alight in the spring with the february-flowering Narcissus pseudonarcissus Praecox'. Features include a pond (with ornamental carp) 'Foxtail Lily Border', the 'Tulip Terrace', where the tulips grow out from boxes of box, a rose garden, an alpine meadow and the national collection of award-winning bearded iris, with around 90 cultivars represented. Huge swags of mistletoe hang from a poplar tree and a magnificent wisteria (planted in 1903) jumbles through a 400 year old yew tree. The racemes on the wisteria, if not caught by a late frost, can be up to 2' long! The 'Lunatic Asylum' was an area where Bowles kept his collection of unusual and bizarre forms of plants (for example the ferox holly and corkscrew hazel) and is due to be restored later this year. The main conservatory is heated and contains tender plants and the coffee machine! The whole garden is being kept up by a small team of gardeners as a continuation of what E.A. Bowles created.
Braille Guide available. Adults: £2; Concessions: £1.40. Plants for sale. Toilets/ and for disabled. Refreshments. Train: Turkey Street + 15mins walk. No dogs allowed. 'Phone for events inluding walks and talks.

22. OSTERLEY PARK
(The National Trust)

daily sunrise- sunset
Isleworth TW7 Tel: 020 8568 7714
The extensive 350 acre landscape of farm and parkland around the Robert Adam house (built in the late 17th century) makes it easy to forget the nearby urban sprawl. The southern half of the park (which is divided by the M4 motorway) contains nearly 150 acres of pleasure grounds and gardens - not bad for a morning stroll, so close to London. There are two large lakes, an arboretum and Pinetum, a cedar lawn and various ornamental built features such as the Garden House and the Temple of Pan. There is a particularly fine Magnolia grandiflora in front of the Old Stables and a diverse selection of tree species including Liquidambar or 'Sweet Gum' which has good autumn colour.
Café & shop(seasonal). Tube: Osterley + 10 mins walk

23. PAINSHILL PARK
(Painshill Park Trust)
Open 11am - 6pm or dusk if earlier. CLOSED mondays (except Bank Hols) & Nov - March fridays as well. Also closed 25 & 26 Dec.
Portsmouth Road, Cobham KT11 1JE Tel: 01932 868 113/ 864 674
160 acres of remarkable landscape garden created from 1738 - 1773, which makes it contemporary with Stourhead in Wiltshire. A large, serpentine lake lies at the centre of the site. Crossing a Chinese Bridge on one side you reach a grotto, parts of which are still

undergoing restoration. Other garden features include an 'amphitheatre' formed by the gradation of different heights and types of shrub; a Turkish Tent, Gothic Tower, waterwheel and Gothick Temple - like Stourhead, this is an eighteenth century Theme park. Many fine specimen trees are throughout, and a tree list is available.

Admission: £4.20; Concession: £3.70; Children (5-16yrs); £1.70. Wheelchairs available.

24. PECKHAM RYE PARK

(London Borough of Southwark)

daily 8am - dusk

Peckham Rye, Southwark SE5 Tel: 0208 693 3791

50 acre Victorian park retaining much of its original layout. There are formal gardens, a rockery, Japanese garden as well as grassland, stream, woodland and conservation areas. There is also an arboretum and a lake.

Visitor Centre; Site partially accessible for wheelchairs; Toilets and for disabled; Train: Peckham Rye

25. STREATHAM COMMON

(London Borough of Lambeth)

daily

Streatham High Road SW16

65 acres of common land with grassland and mature trees. Ornamental pond, flower gardens, paddling pools. Community events take place here.

Café; Toilets; Children's play area. Train: Streatham

Streatham Common - THE ROOKERY

9am - dusk. Closed 25 Dec.

Three acres of garden around what was a private house. The main garden is a walled formal garden, with a wisteria-covered pergola and herbaceous borders. From this you enter the 'White Garden', simple and elegant with white iris' and philadelphus and some nice seating to admire it from. Beyond this is the Orchard area, with grass and picnic tables. Behind the formal garden is a rock garden and a woodland garden with a pond and stream and where, amongst others, azaleas, japanese maples and the giant rhubarb (Gunnera manicata) grow.

Café. Toilets.

26. THAMES BARRIER PARK

(London Development Agency)

daily

North Woolwich Road, Silvertown

A modern landscape design by the French landscape architect Alain Provost, who also designed Parc Andre Citroen in Paris. The site has a strong architectural layout, with a bold water feature and sculpted planting. There is a 'rainbow garden', the 'Green Dock' area, children's play area and a canopy, from which to view the river.

Train: DLR Silvertown

27. TRINITY HOSPICE - Lanning Roper Memorial Garden

(Trustees of the Hospice)

ONLY open 4 w'ends per year (for NGS) and by appt.
30 Clapham Common North Side, London SW4 0RN Tel: Anne Wood on: 0207 787 1000
Two acre garden with a mixture of shrubs and herbaceous plants. The garden was designed by John Medhurst. The link with the American-born garden designer Lanning Roper was that he advised during the early stages of the garden's restoration which began in 1981, although he did not live to see it implemented. There is a romantic over-spill of plants, falling over the edges of borders and cascading over walls. In the large, still pool is a kinetic steel sculpture by George Rickey, and there is a bronze rill and waterfall by William Pye.
Admission: Adults £1; Children free. Toilets/ and for disabled. Teas. Tube: Clapham Common + 10 mins walk.

28. VALENTINES PARK

(London Borough of Redbridge)
8am - dusk
Cranbrook Road
Water features much in this pretty park, with stream, pools, pond and lake. A rather grotty grotto looks down onto the stream, and a small arboretum is in the piece of park oppposite. A very Victorian 'English' garden of box edged borders and a rose garden next door are near the House. Some good ornamental specimen trees throughout. Features of interest are the aviary, boating lake and the ornamental gardens around the 17th century mansion.
Toilets/ and for disabled. Tube: Gants Hill; Train: Ilford

Valentines Park

29. VERNON'S GERANIUM NURSERY

1 March - 31 July including Spring Bank Hols, mon - sat 9.30am - 5.30pm; sun 10am - 4pm.

Cuddington Way, Cheam SM2 7JB Tel: 0208 393 7616

Large nursery specialising in Pelargoniums, Fuchsias, Petunias and other bedding and basket plants. Free open days with tours every day in the last 2 weeks of July at 11am & 2.30pm.

30. WANSTEAD PARK

Northumberland Avenue E12

Daily
This park is now a semi-wild area of 200 acres, once the garden of Wanstead House which was demolished in 1824. The two surviving garden features are an 18th century building known as the 'Temple', and a grotto, built in 1762, now ruined. There is a large lake and an heronry

31. WEST HAM PARK
(Corporation of London)
daily 7.30am - dusk
Upton Lane, Forest Gate E7 9PU Tel: 0208 472 3584
Originally a botanical garden, this 77 acre park now has recreational facilities as well as a seven acre garden in its south east corner. This area of the park includes a rose garden with over 70 different varieties of roses both in the beds and climbing the pergola and encircling trellis. There is a well stocked rock garden, where, amongst others, magnolias, cryptomeria, arbutus and hamamellis provide year-round interest. The nursery provides 300,000 spring and summer bedding plants for this Park as well as other parks and gardens maintained by the Corporation of London.
Toilets & for disabled. Children's playground. Tube: Plaistow

32. WETTERN TREE GARDEN
(London Borough of Croydon)
daily 9am - dusk
Purley Oaks Road, Sanderstead, South Croydon (near the Beech Avenue junction) Tel: 020 8686 4433

Remarkable gardens of just over 1ha. Started in the 1920's by businessman Eric Wettern, the gardens developed with his interest in unusual trees. Now, many varieties of trees and shrubs can be seen, including Siberian Spruce, Coast Redwood, silk tree and many more. Japanese cherries confetti colour in the spring, the delphinium walk and rose gardens pretty in the summer - and the gardens are a blaze of colour in the autumn.

Reasonable access for wheelchairs. Train: Purley Oaks.

APPENDICES

Sites with:

1. Botanical Interest

Chelsea Physic Garden *Area1*
Eccleston Square *Area1*
Holland Park *Area1*
Museum of Garden History *Area1*
Rassell's Nursery *Area 1*
Westminster Abbey - The College Garden *Area1*
Barbican Centre - The Conservatory *Area2*
Columbia Road Flower Market *Area2*
Geffrye Museum Garden *Area2*
Museum of London *Area2*
Clifton Nurseries *Area3*
Hill Garden *Area3*
Regent's Park - Queen Mary's Garden *Area3*
Palm Centre *Area4*
Royal Botanic Gardens, Kew *Area4*
Syon House & Park *Area4*
Capel Manor Gardens *Area5*
City of London Cemetery *Area5*
Hampton Court Palace *Area5*
Jaques Amand International *Area5*
Myddleton House *Area5*
Wettern Tree Garden *Area5*

2. Horticultural Interest

Chelsea Physic Garden *Area1*
Hyde Park - The Rose Garden *Area1*
Kensington Roof Garden *Area1*
Victoria Embankment Gardens *Area1*
Barbican Centre *Area2*
New River Walk *Area2*
Fenton House *Area3*
Regent's Park - Avenue Gardens *Area3*
Chiswick House *Area4*
Ham House *Area4*
Royal Botanic Gardens, Kew *Area4*
Capel Manor Gardens *Area5*
Hampton Court Palace *Area5*
West Ham Park *Area5*

3. Wildlife/ Wildspace

Alexandra Palace *Area3*
Camley Street Natural Park *Area3*
Hampstead Heath *Area3*
Highgate Cemetery *Area3*
Highgate Wood *Area3*
Primrose Hill *Area3*
Barnes Common *Area4*
Richmond Park *Area4*
Wimbledon Common *Area4*
Bushey Park *Area5*
Dulwich Upper Wood Upper Nature Park *Area5*
Epping Forest *Area5*
Greenwich Park *Area5*

Hainault Forest Country Park *Area5*
Osterley Park *Area5*
Wanstead Park *Area5*

4. Landscape/ Garden Design interest
Ebury Square *Area1*
Grosvenor Square *Area1*
Holland Park - Kyoto Garden *Area1*
Kensington Gardens - The Loggia and Italian Garden *Area1*
Kensington Roof Garden *Area1*
Pirelli Garden *Area1*
Ropers Gardens *Area1*
Victoria Embankment - The Whitehall Garden *Area1*
Westminster Abbey - The Little Cloister Garden *Area1*
Barbican Centre *Area2*
Cutler Street Gardens *Area2*
Geffrye Museum Garden *Area2*
New River Walk *Area2*
Burgh House *Area3*
Calthorpe Project *Area3*
Camley Street Natural Park *Area3*
Elthorne Park - Noel Baker Peace Garden *Area3*
Fenton House *Area3*
Hill Garden, The *Area3*
Regent's Park *Area3*
Chiswick House *Area4*
Ham House *Area4*
Claremont Landscape Garden *Area5*

Greenwich Park *Area5*
Hampton Court Palace *Area5*
Painshill Park *Area5*
Thames Barrier Park *Area5*
Trinity Hospice *Area5*

5. Sites with good landscape views
Chelsea Embankment Gardens *Area1*
Cremorne Gardens *Area1*
Hyde Park *Area1*
Kensington Roof Garden *Area1*
St Paul's Cathedral Garden *Area2*
Primrose Hill *Area3*
Chiswick House *Area4*
Furnival Gardens *Area4*
Ham House *Area4*
Marble Hill House *Area4*
Richmond Park *Area 4*
Syon House and Park *Area4*
Wimbledon Common *Area4*
Claremont Landscape Garden *Area5*
Greenwich Park *Area5*
Hainault Forest Country Park *Area5*
Horniman Gardens *Area5*
Island Gardens *Area5*
Osterley Park *Area5*
Painshill Park *Area5*
Thames Barrier Park *Area5*

6. Large! green spaces

Battersea Park *Area1*
Holland Park *Area1*
Hyde Park *Area1*
Kensington Gardens
St James' Park
Victoria Park *Area2*
Alexandra Palace *Area3*
Golders Hill *Area3*
Hampstead Heath *Area3*
Highgate Cemetery *Area3*
Highgate Wood *Area3*
Kenwood House *Area3*
Primrose Hill *Area3*
Queen's Park *Area3*
Regent's Park *Area3*
Waterlow Park *Area3*
Barnes Common *Area4*
Bishop's Park *Area4*
Cannizaro Park *Area4*
Chiswick House *Area4*
Fulham Palace Gardens *Area4*
Gunnerbury Park *Area4*
Ham House *Area4*
Marble Hill House *Area4*
Richmond Park *Area4*
Royal Botanic Gardens, Kew *Area4*
Syon House and Park *Area4*
Wimbledon Common *Area4*
...and most sites in Area 5!

7. Famous or Infamous green spaces to be found in this guide.

Eccleston Square *Area1*
Green Park *Area1*
Hyde Park *Area1*
Kensington Gardens *Area1*
St James' Park *Area1*
Barbican Centre *Area2*
Columbia Road Flower Market *Area2*
Alexandra Palace *Area3*
Fenton House *Area3*
Hampstead Heath *Area3*
Highgate Cemetery *Area3*
Kenwood House *Area3*
Primrose Hill *Area3*
Regent's Park *Area3*
Chiswick House *Area4*
Richmond Park *Area4*
Royal Botanic Gardens, Kew *Area4*
Syon House and Park *Area4*
Wimbledon Common *Area4*
Clapham Common *Area5*
Crystal Palace Park *Area5*
Epping Forest *Area5*
Greenwich Park *Area5*
Hampton Court Palace *Area5*
Thames Barrier Park *Area5*

8. Sites with Historic interest/ notable architecture

Grosvenor Square *Area1*
Kensington Gardens *Area1*
Victoria Embankment Gardens *Area1*
Westminster Abbey *Area1*
Barbican Centre *Area2*
Cutler Street Gardens *Area2*
St Dunstan in the East *Area2*
St Paul's Cathedral Garden *Area2*
Alexandra Palace *Area3*
Emslie Horniman Pleasance *Area3*
Fenton House *Area3*
Highgate Cemetery *Area3*
Hill Garden, The *Area3*
Regent's Park *Area3*
Chiswick House *Area4*
Fulham Palace Gardens *Area4*
Gunnersbury Park *Area4*
Ham House *Area4*
Marble Hill House *Area4*
Royal Botanic Gardens, Kew *Area4*
Syon House and Park *Area4*
City of London Cemetery *Area5*
Claremont Landscape Garden *Area5*
Crystal Palace Park *Area5*
Greenwich Park *Area5*
Hampton Court Palace *Area5*
Horniman Gardens *Area5*
Painshill Park *Area5*
Thames Barrier Park *Area5*

INDEX